PENGUIN BOOKS

THE STATUE OF LIBERTY

Marvin Trachtenberg studied first at Yale
and then at the Institute of Fine Arts
of New York University, where he is now
an Associate Professor. A frequent contributor
to journals in the fields of Italian medieval
and Renaissance art, he is the author of a
monograph, *The Campanile of Florence Cathedral,*
"Giotto's Tower," which was granted the
Alice Davis Hitchcock award by the Society of
Architectural Historians, and is currently
at work on books on Brunelleschi and on
Tuscan Gothic architecture. A visit to
the Statue of Liberty with his two young sons
inspired him to research and write its history.

*Frédéric Auguste Bartholdi was born in Colmar on 2 August 1834 and died
on 4 October 1904 in Paris. He was brought up by his mother in Paris, as his
father, a prosperous civil servant, had died young. After studying architecture he
turned to painting, under Ary Scheffer, and sculpture in the studios of
Jean-François Soitoux and Antoine Etex. He made his name at the Exposition
Universelle of 1855 in Paris with a bronze statue of General Rapp for Colmar.
In 1856 he went to Egypt with the painter J.-L. Gérôme and in 1869 went there
again in the hope of obtaining a commission for a colossal statue to commemorate the
opening of the Suez Canal. In 1870 he served as an officer in the Franco-Prussian
War and much of his subsequent career was devoted to the execution of war
memorials, notably the huge red sandstone Lion of Belfort (1875–80). His other
main theme was the relationship between France and the United States expressed
in statues of Lafayette (Salon of 1873 and now in Union Square, New York)
and the bronze group of Washington and Lafayette (Salon of 1892 and now in
the Place des États-Unis, Paris) as well as* The Statue of Liberty.
He visited America four times, in 1871, 1876, 1886 and 1893.

The Statue of Liberty *originally entitled* Liberty Enlightening the World
(La Liberté éclairant le monde*), is constructed of a hammered copper shell, 2.5 mm
thick, attached by trusswork to a wrought-iron pylon designed by Gustave Eiffel,
mounted on a 27 meter stone and concrete pedestal designed by Richard M. Hunt, on
Liberty (originally Bedloe's) Island, New York. The statue is 46 meters high from
the base to the top of the torch, 34 meters from heel to top of the head. Bartholdi's
surviving models date from 1870–75 (Musée Bartholdi, Colmar, and the Museum
of the City of New York, New York). The statue was completed in the Paris
workshops of Gaget, Gauthier et Cie. in 1884 and was shipped to New York the
following year. It was unveiled on 26 October 1886.*

PENGUIN BOOKS

The Statue of Liberty

Marvin Trachtenberg

Penguin Books Ltd, Harmondsworth,
Middlesex, England
Penguin Books, 625 Madison Avenue,
New York, New York 10022, U.S.A.
Penguin Books Australia Ltd, Ringwood,
Victoria, Australia
Penguin Books Canada Ltd, 2801 John Street,
Markham, Ontario, Canada L3R 1B4
Penguin Books (N.Z.) Ltd, 182–190 Wairau Road,
Auckland 10, New Zealand

First published in Great Britain by Allen Lane 1974
First published in the United States of America
by The Viking Press 1976
Published in Penguin Books 1977

LIBRARY OF CONGRESS CATALOGING IN PUBLICATION DATA
Trachtenberg, Marvin
The Statue of Liberty.
Includes bibliographical references.
1. Bartholdi, Frédéric Auguste, 1834–1904.
2. Statue of Liberty, New York.   I. Title.
[NB553.B3T72 1977]   730'.92'4   77–5624
ISBN 0 14 00.4513 9

Printed in the United States of America by
The Book Press, Brattleboro, Vermont
Set in Monophoto Ehrhardt

Edited by John Fleming and Hugh Honour
Designed by Gerald Cinamon and Paul McAlinden

To my mother and the memory of my father

Contents

Historical Table

1869 Suez Canal opened. U.S. Transcontinental railroad completed.

1870 Franco–Prussian War. Dogma of Papal Infallibility.

1871 France loses Alsace and Lorraine. National Assembly. Thiers elected President. Paris Commune.

1874 French protectorate over Annam.

1875 Third Republic.

1876 Bakunin organizes 'Land and Liberty' society.

1877 Macmahon dissolves Chamber: Republicans win election. Hayes government in U.S.A.

1878 Congress of Berlin.

1879 Republicans control French Senate. Grévy elected president. Standard Oil Trust formed.

1880 Amnesty to exiles of Paris Commune. Garfield President of the U.S.

1881 Tunisia becomes French protectorate. President Garfield assassinated.

1882 Triple Alliance of Germany, Austria, Italy.

1883 Ferry's second ministry.

1884 French protectorate over Annam and Tonkin re-established.

1885 Cleveland president of U.S.A.

1886 Bonaparte and Orléans families banished from France.

Bartholdi lighthouse projects for Suez. Brooklyn Bridge begun, completed 1883.	Mark Twain, *Innocents Abroad*; Jules Verne, *20,000 Leagues under the Sea*; Flaubert, *Education Sentimentale*.	1869
Bartholdi's first *Liberty* model.	Wagner: *Die Walküre*.	1870
Bartholdi visits U.S.A. for *Liberty* project. Whistler, *The Artist's Mother*.	Rimbaud, *Le Bateau Ivre*; Whitman, *Democratic Vistas*.	1871
First Impressionist Exhibition.	Wagner's *Ring* completed.	1874
French-American Union organized to sponsor *Liberty*. Bartholdi's final model for *Liberty*. Bartholdi begins *Lion of Belfort*, completed 1880.		1875

Liberty's arm and torch exhibited at Philadelphia. The Albert Memorial completed.	E. Lesbazeilles, *Les Colosses anciens et modernes*; Mallarmé, *L'Après-midi d'un faune*; Brahms's First Symphony; Gounod, 'Liberty Cantata'.	1876
U.S. Congress accepts gift of *Liberty*. Third Impressionist Exhibition.	Henry James, *The American*.	1877
Liberty's head at Paris Fair. Rodin, *The Walking Man*.		1878
Viollet-le-Duc dies. Eiffel begins Garabit Bridge, completed 1884, and becomes *Liberty* engineer.	Ibsen, *A Doll's House*.	1879
Bartholdi, *Liberty* pedestal project.	Zola, *Nana*. Dostoyevsky, *The Brothers Karamazov*.	1880

100,000 French contributors, including 181 towns, raise funds for *Liberty*'s fabrication. Rodin's *Gates of Hell* begun.	Henry James, *The Portrait of a Lady*.	1881
Hunt's first design for *Liberty*'s pedestal. Manet, *The Bar at the Folies-Bergère*.	Whitman, *Specimen Days*; Wagner, *Parsifal*.	1882
Laboulaye dies. De Lesseps leads French-American Union for *Liberty*. Ground broken for pedestal. Jenney's Home Life Insurance Building, Chicago, introduces skyscraper construction.	Nietzsche, *Thus Spake Zarathustra*.	1883
Liberty presented to the U.S. at Paris ceremony. Cornerstone laid on completed foundation. Rodin, *Burghers of Calais*.	Mark Twain, *Huckleberry Finn*; H. Spencer, *The Man versus the State*.	1884
Liberty arrives in New York. $100,000 raised for the pedestal by the New York *World*.	Zola, *Germinal*; Marx, *Das Kapital* vol. 2 published posthumously.	1885

Liberty unveiled. Seurat, *La Grande Jatte*.	Jean Moréas, manifesto of literary symbolism. Nietzsche, *Beyond Good and Evil*; Krafft-Ebing, *Psychopathia Sexualis*.	1886

Acknowledgements

This study would never have appeared were it not for the initial enthusiasm of my friend Richard Pommer, and even more the editors, John Fleming and Hugh Honour, who took the idea more seriously than I did, commissioned the work and nursed it in various ways over what must have seemed an interminable time. Institutional personnel were unusually helpful, in particular M. Pierre Burger of the Musée Bartholdi in Colmar and Mr John Bond, Mr Robert Rothe, and Mr Lewis Morris of the National Park Service in New York. My colleagues, Professors Henry-Russell Hitchcock, Isabelle Hyman, H. W. Janson, and Robert Rosenblum were kind enough to read the manuscript and offer invaluable criticism. Others who contributed information or suggestions include M. Jacques Betz, Mr Allan Burnham, Mr Henry Hope Reed, Dr Manfred Fischer, Professors P. H. von Blanckenhagen, Colin Eisler, Robert Mark, Donald Posner, Kathleen Weil-Garris Posner, Gert Schiff, Renate Wagner-Rieger, and David van Zanten. I am grateful to the Institute of Fine Arts for a research leave and for its many enthusiastic students who deluged me with a stream of information about things relating to the statue, among them Mr Nicholas Adams and Miss Eleanor Pearson, the most unsparing. Particularly helpful in providing photographs were Professor Dr Margarete Kühn, Professor Dr P. Dubas (Zurich), Professor Dr Martin Warnke, the firm of Fotostampa Reggiori (Laveno M. [Varese]), the New York Historical Society, and the Library of Congress. Finally, I owe a debt to my two sons who got me started

14

by enticing me out to the statue one fine Sunday three years ago; and to my wife, Heidi, for her assistance in research, travel and with the manuscript, and her enduring patience living with a mono-graphist.

M.T.
New York

Introduction

Just what makes a monument? Everyone knows, as Marcel
Duchamp discovered, that one has only to place a plumbing fixture
in a museum gallery and it becomes a work of art. But placing a
work of art in a city square does not necessarily make it a monument;
it may merely make a museum of the square. The Latin root of the
word means 'things that remind'. This involves more than simply
tombs and memorials. Monuments are public, permanent visual
structures – traditionally sculpture, architecture, or both, and
sometimes painting – that are intended to symbolize something
generally shared by a group or even an entire society (although
'private' monuments are not unknown). They stand for common
ideas, memories, and hopes. They mark the men and events chosen
by a society as part of its image. They express its traumas of
growth and suffering and its pride of accomplishment. In a broader
sense, monuments function as social magnets, crystalizations of
social energy, one of the means civilization has devised to reinforce
its cohesiveness and to give meaning and structure to life. Monuments are a way men transmit communal emotions, a medium of
continuity and interaction between generations, not only in space
but across time, for to be monumental is to be permanent. They
may serve other ends as well – of a functional, visual, or urban
nature, or of artistic self-expression – but not in their primary
capacity.

Monuments are unfashionable today. We hardly build any new
ones and the old ones are ignored, satirized, and sometimes even
destroyed. We evidently don't want to be 'reminded' any longer,

at least not in the old way, either about the events of our times or about those of the past. The fine arts that gave monuments form in the past have gone their separate ways, and few artists could now accept a commission for a true monument in good faith, for, as Rodin already had discovered, modernism appears to exclude authentic monument making. The old creative tension between artistic self-expression and the social content of the monument has become antithesis, and, in any case, the public's desire for their union has disappeared.

Yet, strangely, the *Statue of Liberty* has today attained a general prominence that it has not had since the time of its unveiling, almost as if to receive the accumulated attention denied other monuments. Hardly a season passes without *Liberty* being adopted by some party (such as the recent peace demonstrators), and hardly a day goes by without an appearance in the media, often for banal commercial ends but not infrequently expressing strong feelings about America's nature, its problems and hopes. Officially it is but another national monument. Yet in the popular imagination the *Statue of Liberty* is the symbolic image of America, more than Washington's profile, the eagle, or even the Flag. She receives due reverence, even idolization from the millions who flock to visit her each year. And among the intelligentsia *Liberty* is at least notorious. She has become more than just another pop-object, like an Andy Warhol soup can or soap box. If anything, she is the very queen of Pop Art, so elevated in that realm of high satire that she but rarely appears in Pop works. Like a true royal figure, she is everywhere even when unseen.

Unlike other monumental victims of our times, *Liberty* would appear miraculously to have been kept alive by some historical alchemy. Yet the 'great lady', now nearly a century old, is not what she once was. She has dissolved so much into an image and even more into a symbol, that it is only with difficulty (as Ernst Gombrich has noted) that the visitor to the statue can see her as such at all, let alone as the 'autograph' work of an otherwise forgotten artist.[1] And, indeed, what today's spectator sees in *Liberty* is scarcely what she meant to her makers and early public.

Part of *Liberty*'s lost significance was simply her status as just one among many monuments – a large and unusual one, to be sure – in an age of monument building. If our day marks its nadir, the nineteenth century (and early twentieth century) was the heyday of the monument. So extravagant was its flowering, in every conceivable form, from the Washington Monument to the Albert Memorial, and in nearly every center of western civilization, from London to Leningrad to Hanoi (a French colonial capital where a *Liberty* copy was set up), that much of our present attitude might be interpreted, in part, as a reaction to the excesses of the past. Any public personage, event, memory, aspiration, virtue, occupation, or preoccupation occasioned at least one project for a monument that, more often than not, had a good chance of being erected. The slightest pretext would suffice, and memorials sprang up like an army of bronze and marble. Many aspects of the era contributed to this phenomenon: the great new wealth, materialism, and pride; nationalism and local patriotism, and the increasing pomposity of life style; the visual role of monuments in the extensive urban rebuilding and embellishment of the age. So compulsive, however, even pathological, does the scene appear in retrospect that it is almost as if the production of monuments served also as a kind of cultural device for relieving the pressures of the puffed-up age. Only the prevalence of this phenomenon can explain how it was possible for *Liberty*'s sponsors to conceive of erecting such a work.

This is only again to suggest the disparity – even the antithesis – between *Liberty* then and now, and the nature of the former. Naturally there is no question of bringing *Liberty* and her times back. But even to travel back to *Liberty* in the historical imagination is difficult, for her story has been lost, not only in the popular memory – where it was understandably obscured in the process of transforming *Liberty*'s meaning – but in art-historical scholarship, which has disdained *Liberty* through an evident confusion of museum art and the monument and a judging of all such artifacts by the criteria of the former.

To restore *Liberty*'s lost historical tissue of circumstance, form and meaning is the first task of any serious study of the statue. This is, of course, true of all art-historical studies, but the case here is different. Art-historical writings are normally about inherently impressive and, most frequently, strikingly beautiful works, and understandably center on the object itself: its form, chronology, position in the artist's oeuvre, iconography and, when relevant, something of patronage and the relationship to historical events. Whatever the composition of the monograph the object itself tends to remain visible and prominent throughout. This approach raises difficulties for the student of *Liberty*. She is presentable, in fact, eminently so for the scale at which a classically draped human form is rendered, and her convincing dignity is reinforced by her truly impressive pedestal. But she is no great sculptural beauty, and she never was. In fact, *Liberty*'s form – removed from the site and context and reduced to ordinary size – would really be of little intrinsic interest to anyone except perhaps the pedantic specialist and the manufacturers of souvenir models. This singularity, coupled with the significance and complexity of *Liberty* as a monument, has led me to give this study an inverted structure. *Liberty*'s sculptural style does find a certain place – she is, after all, still a work of sculpture designed by a particular artist at a given moment. Yet what is of most interest about the monument is everything but pure sculptural form: *Liberty*'s origins, patronage, and public; symbolism, colossal scale, and spectacular setting. There are her multiple authors; the remarkable pedestal – itself an architectural colossus – and the even more remarkable interior structure, which grandly uplift and firmly support the huge sculptural form; and the place of all these in the culture and history of the period.

If this approach tends to yield a broken image of the monument, it is the result not only of the statue's formal vacuity. It is appropriate to what was an age of eclecticism, of the fragmentation of meaning and experience, of the analysis of the process of making and the increasing specialization of skills in every pursuit. In the final analysis the *Statue of Liberty* is an archetypal embodiment of these tendencies.

1. Unveiling the *Statue of Liberty*, 28 October 1886

1. The Circumstances

As the unveiling ceremony droned on far below on a wet, foggy October afternoon of 1886, Auguste Bartholdi waited impatiently inside the head of his statue of *Liberty Enlightening the World* to loose her unveiling cords [1]. The Parisian sculptor was a sentimental man, and, gazing through the diadem windows overlooking the great harbor, he may have recalled the bright day fifteen years earlier when his laborious romance with the New World began. It had been in June 1871 that Bartholdi first sailed into New York harbor bearing with him a grandiose sculptural vision. Although, improbably realized, the monument was to make him famous, it was more than an artist's ambition that accounted for his long journey. Bartholdi's fortunes were entangled in the web of mid-nineteenth-century politics. Its spinning makes a tale that has often been told, but never fully, for *Liberty*'s chroniclers and poets have usually succumbed to the lure of patriotic myth-making – French and American – rather than confront the hard and not always appealing historical facts.[1]

In the backward-looking, smug world of the annual Paris Salon and state-sponsored art Frédéric Auguste Bartholdi, having made his first splash in the 1853 season at the precocious age of nineteen, cut something of a figure by the 1860s. An academic master of typically unimpressive talent, but unsurpassed as a promoter of his own ambitious sculptural schemes, Bartholdi had made his name in the glut of monument building in the prosperous cities of Second Empire France.[2] Suddenly, however, this favorable tide of circumstance seemed to ebb. The France of June 1871 was barren ground for public monuments. The final act of a national catastrophe was being played out: military humiliation and a degrading peace at the hands of the new Germany (and the loss of Bartholdi's native Alsace); the collapse of the Second Empire, with Napoleon III and his court in flight; Paris ravaged by the *Commune*, its streets flowing with the blood of reprisal as Bartholdi left to cross the Atlantic.

It was not as a political *émigré* that Bartholdi visited the United States in 1871 nor as an artist primarily in search of new commissions (although that was an activity he never neglected). Yet both politics and a new commission were involved in his voyage. Its purpose was to explore and promote the project for a monument to be donated by the citizens of France to the United States, with matching American funds to set it up, to commemorate the approaching centennial of 1776. This project was not entirely, nor even predominantly, Bartholdi's own. Nor was he acting on behalf of the spontaneous generosity of the French nation, as is commonly believed. He was sent to America in 1871 as the agent of a small group of activist French intellectuals of moderate republican stamp who had something more specific in mind than international cordiality. Édouard-René Lefebvre de Laboulaye (1811–83) was the principal figure in this circle.[3] It was at his dinner table that the project for the *Statue of Liberty* was first discussed and he may well be considered its father.

To be properly understood, the origins of the *Statue of Liberty* must be seen in the context of French politics in the 1860s and early 1870s,[4] French notions of liberty and republicanism (both associated with the image of the United States [2]), and especially Laboulaye's political philosophy. For although the statue was destined to become a personification of the United States, it began as an expression of French ideas. The project for its erection in New York Harbor was, moreover, a French political ploy.

Laboulaye's career provides an easily identifiable thread running through the tangled skein of French politics in the last years of the

2. *Le Docteur Francklin couronné par la Liberté.*
J. C. R. de Saint-Non
after Fragonard, *c.* 1780

Second Empire and the first of the Third Republic.[5] An internationally distinguished jurist, he had been since 1849 Professor of Comparative Legislation at the Collège de France where his wit and imagination, no less than his strong republican convictions, made him a popular lecturer. His political outlook led him, early in his career, to the study of the great modern exemplar of republicanism, the United States. And after the death of de Tocqueville in 1859 he emerged as the leading French authority on American constitutional history. A prolific writer, he published a three-volume *Histoire des États-Unis* (1855–66), and a satirical story about a Parisian suddenly transported into an ongoing New York existence, *Paris in America* (1863), besides numerous tracts and articles which included a plea for the cause of the Union against the South, first published in the *Journal des débats* in 1862, translated into English and frequently reprinted in America. A scholarly nature, a retiring disposition and delicate health kept him from the center stage of French politics for most of his life. But he played a not inconsequential role in the last months of Napoleon III's reign when he somewhat surprisingly compromised his principles by giving support to the regime in the hope of liberalizing it. After 1870 he was, however, to salvage his reputation and to emerge within the charmed circle of republican leadership in the National Assembly. Although never a dominant public figure he contributed materially to his party's ultimate ascendancy.

The political situation in 1871 was characterized by Laboulaye as 'a moment when a bewildered France searches for its way but does not find it'.[6] The instability of the French state since 1789 had acquired the appearance of a permanent condition. A succession of regimes, unwilling and unable to create true political equilibrium, had maintained only an appearance of stability and order by stifling opposition. But the ideas and energies released by the Revolution were not to be contained. Splinters of revolution continued to smolder beneath the surface after the restoration of the monarchy in 1815 and burst into flame at regular two-decade intervals – in 1830, 1848 and 1871. A monstrous political cycle seemed to have been established in a nation viciously divided against itself [3].

Under the Second Empire, even before the liberalization of press censorship in 1868, there were always indirect means for the opposition to express itself. A common literary device was to explore subjects distant in place or time in a manner calculated to make the reader reflect on contemporary conditions at home.[7] The Emperor himself had resorted to such a mode of expression in his study of Caesar in the mid-1860s, asserting an autocratic ideology

3. *Apparition du serpent de mer en 1848.*
By Cham,
in *Charivari*, 23 December 1848

by reference to the Hegelian concept of the man of destiny –
Caesar, Charlemagne or Napoleon I – who appears at a critical
moment to save society and restore the authority of the state.[8]

For the opposition America was a primary theme. Since its dis-
covery, the New World had provided a region for the utopian
dreams of many polemicists, the more notable including Voltaire
and, in his more moderate way, de Tocqueville. Indeed, after 1776,
America was often seen by the French as the realization of the
political philosophy of the Enlightenment, the embodiment of
Liberty and Reason. By the mid-1860s the United States – particularly after the victory of the Union – was the ascendant republic.
And the French recalled that they had shared in its launching.
Washington and Lafayette were still paired in patriotic speeches
on both sides of the Atlantic. More specifically, the success of
America appeared to the French as a synthesis of principles which
seemed doomed for ever to incompatibility in their own country –
order and liberty.[9]

Laboulaye was a leading practitioner of the use of the American example to criticise home policy. Of his major works, mainly written under the censorship of the Second Empire, none was of purely scholarly motivation. All of them involved some degree of political intent and nearly all had the same theme, whether cast as a *History of the United States* – written with the avowed purpose of discovering the 'durable conditions of liberty' and presenting as a great revolutionary hero not Napoleon but Washington 'who reconciled the world with Liberty' – or as *Paris in America*, his still amusing satire of French attitudes to things American, especially liberty.[10] Perhaps the most intense of his American writings – and the most relevant to our subject – was the widely circulated tract which he wrote in 1862 when the success of the Union was in doubt and the French were divided as to which (if either) side to aid. 'Frenchmen, who have not forgotten Lafayette nor the glorious memories we left behind in the new world – it is your cause which is on trial in the United States,' he wrote. 'This cause has been defended by energetic men for a year with equal courage and ability; our duty is to range ourselves round them, and to hold aloft with a firm hand that old French banner, on which is inscribed, Liberty.'[11]

Thus there is no reason to doubt the inner truth of Bartholdi's account (although written for fund-raising purposes in 1885) of the origins of the *Statue of Liberty* in a discussion about America at Laboulaye's dinner table at his estate at Glatigny (near Versailles) in 1865.[12] Bartholdi was included in the gathering, attended by a number of his eventual backers, probably as a result of a portrait commission.[13] He reports that after dinner the question of gratitude between nations arose, and that Laboulaye distinguished between the play of power politics in most international relations, such as those between France and Italy, and the 'wholly different thing in the case of other nations or peoples with whom there was a genuine flow of sympathy, caused, it might be, by experiences common to the two nations, it might be by affinity of aspiration, or by the influence of certain feelings which served as a bond of union.'

Such was manifestly the case of the United States and France, he continued. Indeed, he went on to say that 'if a monument were to be built in America as a memorial to . . . independence, I should think it very natural if it were built by united effort, if it were a common work of both nations.'

Laboulaye's reputed words, regardless of historical accuracy, contain much wishful thinking and exaggeration of an international friendship. In actuality, such fragile sentiments were overshadowed by emotions concerning national affairs. If any strong feelings were projected abroad, it was hatred of enemies. Moreover, during the Civil War, the French government had exploited the American inability to respond to the Mexican venture of Maximilian. Yet the old myth of alliance proved enduring; at least there remained enough good will and attachment to revolutionary memories to make the scheme of a common Franco-American monument seem workable to Laboulaye and his colleagues, particularly if their own efforts could bring about the initial gift across the sea. The monument as propaganda – particularly prevalent in France during and after the Revolution – was as old as the pyramids; but here for once it was to serve not the establishment, but the opposition.

The idealistic, and rather fervent tone of Laboulaye's gathering – as described by Bartholdi – was characteristic not only of the generation of men at it, but, with respect to America, particularly of the year 1865. The assassination of Lincoln, following on the triumph of the Republic and its projection of libertarian hopes, produced an outpouring of French sentiment, no less, it seems, than a mass catharsis. These feelings are recorded in numerous letters sent to the American representative in Paris (and preserved by John Bigelow, who was to become an important intermediary in the communications of the statue organizers) from all parts of France, and from Frenchmen in all walks of life although principally from republicans and liberal monarchists. One such letter, signed by the people of Caen, declared that America's 'sorrow is the sorrow of all good men' because Lincoln had met his tasks and overcome them 'without veiling the statue of Liberty'. French republicans lost no time in making political capital of the situation. A project was supported, if not initiated, through the newspaper *Phare de la Loire* for a medal honoring Lincoln to be struck in gold and presented to his widow. The public subscription that was begun, however, was quickly confiscated by Napoleon's agents and the lists of supporters destroyed. Nevertheless, by the end of 1866 the medal was in the grateful hands of Mrs Lincoln, the profile bust of her husband on the obverse bearing the inscription 'Dedicated by the French Democracy to Lincoln' and including on the reverse in bold letters the motto 'Liberty, Equality, Fraternity'.[14]

The twenty-six eminent republicans – including Michelet, Louis Blanc, Hugo – who signed the covering letter and who claimed to be speaking for 40,000 Frenchmen surely would have desired a grander monument. But even the innocuous medal had to be struck in Switzerland and smuggled into France to the American embassy which passed it on to its ultimate destination in the diplomatic bag. The time was not yet ripe for the kind of monumental commemoration Laboulaye had in mind in 1865. Nor was it yet in 1868 when, sparking off a controversy which came to be known as 'l'affaire Baudin' (after one of the 'martyrs'), the fiery republican Gambetta proposed a national monument to his compatriots who fell in the 1848 revolution.[15] Yet, looking back, it is clear that in the Lincoln medal at least some kind of precedent had been set.

But ideas were soon to be overtaken by events in France. The country had been invaded, defeated, humiliated by Prussia. In February 1871 the French elected a provisional assembly to make peace terms and to determine a permanent form of government. From the overwhelmingly conservative initial composition of this body it would have seemed that a return to some form of kingship was in store for France – as in the late 1790s, 1815, 1830 and 1853. But the conservatives were bitterly divided between themselves and there were two contenders for the crown, the Bourbon comte de Chambord and the Orleanist comte de Paris. For a short while it seemed that a compromise might be reached by giving the crown first to the comte de Chambord (grandson of Charles X) who had no heir and from whom it could then pass to the more politically aggressive comte de Paris. In the event, however, the comte de Chambord, though he paid lip-service to some constitutional ideas, refused to accept the Tricolor (in place of the Bourbon *fleur-de-lis*) as the national flag, either in 1871 or, decisively, in 1873 when the monarchist cause was finally lost.

Meanwhile moderate republicans had been gathering strength. In the past forty years their image had been repeatedly damaged by the excesses of extremists – in 1832–5, 1848 and 1871. But as a result the moderates were now able to take control of the party. In supplementary elections beginning as early as July 1871, they gradually eroded the conservative majority as the electorate slowly threw off the hold of the establishment and rejected any return to the *ancien régime*. But to create a government they needed help – as Laboulaye remarked in 1871, 'the establishment of the Republic will not be the work of one party'.[16] The moderate republicans thus shrewdly turned to the liberal monarchists who were increasingly disenchanted with the infighting of the two pretenders and their immediate supporters. As the 1870s wore on, moreover, Bonapartism threatened to rise like a phoenix from the ashes – and this the monarchists dreaded even more than they feared Republicanism. To attract these anxious monarchists, the moderate – 'conservative' as they styled themselves – republicans took great pains to maintain an image of respectability, refraining from attacks on the Church and avoiding any suggestion that they stood for radical social reform.

By late 1874 a center-left coalition of moderate monarchists and conservative republicans achieved ascendancy. On 28 January 1875 Laboulaye – later to be made a life senator for his contribution to the new regime – made an impassioned speech on a motion to establish a republic and almost carried the house. Two days later,

the chamber accepted a proposal – the famous Wallon Amendment –
that indirectly, but unequivocally, recognized a republican status
in France. After this turning point events followed quickly.
Refraining from attempting the creation of a full constitution,
which would have shattered the coalition, the republicans forced
through a series of constitutional laws (ingeniously framed by a
committee in which Laboulaye, as an academic authority on such
matters, played a key role). The cumulative result was the Third
Republic. By December, its work done, the provisional assembly
was dissolved and the new regime officially began. Unwilling to
give up, the Orleanists forced elections in 1877 and spared no pains
to rig them. But they merely set the stage for the clearest triumph
of the republicans – an overwhelming majority of 340 to 200.
Although threats lingered on, the French government was to
remain steadfastly republican until a second German occupation
in the 1940s.

It was in the highly charged French political atmosphere of 1871
that the idea of the *Statue of Liberty* first became a serious possibility. The moderate republicans saw that every possible means
was needed to advance their cause. What better way to increase the
chances of their ultimate victory than by fortifying the republican
image of France? And what better means was there to accomplish
this than with a truly grandiose monument linking the history and
destiny of France with the great modern republican state, the
America that had not only triumphed over its internal enemies but
was ascendant in every sphere, already marked to be one of the
great world powers? If the monarchists had lost their cause by
adherence to a flag – the republicans might succeed with the help
of a weightier symbol.

Laboulaye had been grooming Bartholdi for this task since 1865.
Bartholdi's letters to his mother in December 1869 contain cryptic
references to 'my American' and speak of his hopes concerning
'this project'.[17] Already in June 1870, when the regime of Napoleon

III was faltering, an exploratory trip to America was proposed, as Bartholdi indicates in a letter to his mother (2 June) 'concerning the dream of America . . .'[18] In those months he spent part of the time in his Paris studio working on preliminary ideas for this project, a stage of its development preserved in a single clay maquette [17] in the Musée Bartholdi at Colmar (signed and dated 1870). A year later he was on his way to New York armed with instructions and letters of introduction from Laboulaye, who a month earlier at another political meeting at Glatigny had told him (as Bartholdi recalled it in 1885) 'that without any doubt there would be at the hundredth anniversary of the Independence of the United States a movement patriotic and French in America. "Go to see that country," said he to me. "You will study it, you will bring back to us your impressions. Propose to our friends over there to make with us a monument, a common work, in remembrance of the ancient friendship of France and the United States. We will take up a subscription in France. If you find a happy idea, a plan that will excite public enthusiasm, we are convinced that it will be successful on both continents, and we will do a work that will have a far-reaching moral effect."' Before leaving, Bartholdi wrote to Laboulaye (8 May) 'I will try to glorify the Republic and Liberty over there, in the hope that someday I will find it again here . . .'[19]

Bartholdi's trip lasted the whole summer. To judge by his letters and other writings, America never had a more enthusiastic visitor, making the acquaintance of its liberal leaders (including Laboulaye's friend, the great abolitionist, Senator Sumner), monied potential backers, newspaper publishers, and even President Grant; travelling 'from the East to the West, and from the North to the South', taking in everything with a keen eye; but above all else talking about and proselytizing his project (even dauntlessly in Salt Lake City).[20] He met with sufficient positive response – or so he pretended – to justify an enthusiastic report to his backers on his return to France. He had found a site – Bedloe's Island in

New York harbor, astride the very gateway to the new world. He had been given reason to hope that Congress could be persuaded to approve his plans. The spectacular location was to bear a monument of proportionate ambition; its program, we shall discover, may have already been in the makings as early as 1870, but it appears to have taken definite shape only during his journey across America. And at a meeting convened at Glatigny in the fall of 1871 to hear about his voyage, Bartholdi affirmed the idea. Laboulaye had recently written, 'Progress is nothing but Liberty in action.'[21] Now the theme of Bartholdi's monument, according to Laboulaye's colleague, the historian Henri Martin, was to be 'a sublime phrase which sums up the progress of modern times: "Liberty Enlightening the World,"' to be represented 'by a statue of colossal proportions which would surpass all that have ever existed since the most ancient times.'[22]

Whatever groundwork had been accomplished in 1871 the project had to wait some time for fruition. Although eager to hear of his progress, Bartholdi's colleagues were fully absorbed in the intense, sustained political struggle at home by the time he returned from America. But it was not only a question of priorities. Caution was the watchword of these republicans: precipitous action was to be avoided at all costs. Let Bartholdi work out the final model; let the word be spread; then wait and see what happens in the political arena. The idea was to keep the project as a trump to be played when all the cards were down.

Thus Bartholdi had to wait almost half a decade before the project was made public. Meanwhile, there was a testing of the intended mode of propaganda with a less pretentious, and correspondingly less dangerous work. In 1873 Thiers, a constitutional monarchist who had by then moved very close to the moderate republicans, in the closing months of his presidential office commissioned Bartholdi to execute a larger than life bronze statue of Lafayette to be given to the city of New York for its aid to Paris after the suffering of the siege of the winter of 1870–71. Exhibited in plaster in the Salon of 1873, it was as non-partisan a political gesture as could be conceived, and, upon its delivery and erection in Union Square three years later during the centennial, it was a substantial success [59].

French political observers consequently were not shocked when, in 1875, simultaneously with the triumph of the moderate republicans, the project of Laboulaye and Bartholdi surfaced with a great fanfare. A so-called French-American Union was established (with Laboulaye at the head of the French side) to raise funds on both sides of the Atlantic and to coordinate publicity and other matters.[23] Public announcements, begun late in 1874, reached a climax with a festive banquet at the Hôtel du Louvre on 6 November 1875, less than a month before the work of the republicans was accomplished and the constitutional assembly dissolved. The banquet was attended not only by an honor roll of the center-left, but also by more conservative members of the executive.[24] That the project met with acceptance from such a wide range of the political spectrum forms part of our picture of the operations of the liberals, who, as we have seen, had judiciously concentrated on the means of gathering France around them.

Shrewd observers of this scene might have perceived that the strategy of the promoters included an evasive tactic concerning the genesis of the program of the monument. In complementary disclaimers, Laboulaye attributed the idea to Bartholdi's imagination,[25] just as Bartholdi was to remember it as the inspiration of Laboulaye. The intention was for the statue to appear as impersonal in origin, as natural in theme, and as universal in appeal as possible. However, although it is difficult to prove conclusively, it is hard to imagine that it was not the patron who played the main role. Laboulaye, an older man whom Bartholdi appears to have revered, was not merely the guiding spirit of the whole effort. The monument's theme issues directly from the core of his political ideology. In Laboulaye's writings Liberty recurs as a *leitmotif* – indeed, forms an underlying structural idea. 'God and Liberty' (Voltaire's famous blessing on the head of Franklin's grandson) is even the motto of his American history (and fittingly, for in actual practice his libertarianism – like his colleagues' – was moderate and certainly without any taint of radical socialism).[26] But it must be added that he had enough wit to see his position clearly, even caricaturing himself as the Frenchman in his *Paris in America*, who, returning to France 'thinks and speaks only of liberty' and who, when finally considered a madman, defends himself in a most Gallic manner in the closing lines of the book: 'The madness of love is cured when one is young; if old one dies of it; the madness of ambition yields sometimes to age and the contempt of mankind; the madness of liberty is never cured.'

Although extreme in his devotion to the ideal (as had been his illustrious predecessor, de Tocqueville), Laboulaye was certainly not alone. Liberty was not only a banner for liberals. A good part of its fitness for the monument was the fact that the times knew no more universal political theme. In fact, it was such a *sine qua non* of nineteenth-century French political ideology that (like today) even its enemies paid it lip service. Napoleon III, writing of his famous uncle in *Les Idées Napoléoniennes* of 1839, proclaimed in an Orwellian manner, 'His aim was liberty, yes *liberty*.'[27] Under his reign and well into the Third Republic, the Church battled for 'Liberty of Education', by which it meant, of course, license to control the tutelage of the masses. But even in the Church there was a detectable movement, from Pius's *Syllabus of Errors* of 1864 to the rather more conciliatory Bull of Leo XIII, *Libertas* of 1888, which gave a nodding acceptance to the Republic. On all sides liberty was a theme that demanded public acquiescence – so much so, in fact, that it is now rather difficult to determine the precise contemporary political implications of the image. In a series of cartoons published during the Commune of 1871, for example, 'Liberty' is shown in various stages of the Passion – crucified before a map of France on the title-page [4]. But by the mid-1870s the republicans clearly saw Liberty as a possible lever

4. *La Grande Crucifiée*.
Courtaux, 1871

to help change the structure of France, given sufficient length and a position for the fulcrum. The political victory of 1875 provided just this needed pivotal support; the colossus of *Liberty*, at the end of a long lever arm, should provide added momentum to events.

Yet there was a good deal more to the project than shrewd calculation. Liberty was, after all, not only politically expedient as a theme, but perfectly natural for any Franco-American monument – being, obviously, the common denominator between '*Liberté, Égalité, Fraternité*' and 'Life, liberty, and the pursuit of

Le
Petit Journal

7000000

5 centimes

Dargaud

happiness'. But it is very significant, nevertheless, that *Liberty*'s first public appearance should have coincided with its patrons' political victory: quite clearly *it* was meant, not originally but certainly in 1875, as a monument celebrating that very triumph. Liberty, 'enlightening the world' from the shores of America, had at least tentatively won in France – as Gounod's 'Liberty Cantata' of 1876 proclaimed (albeit referring primarily to America)[28] – and the statue was to celebrate that event also.

Why not then erect the colossus in Paris? After seeing her set up at the Parisian workshop before shipment to New York in 1885 Parisians certainly regretted having to relinquish her [5, 79]; and shortly afterwards a copy at a quarter-scale was erected on the Île des Cygnes [6] downstream from the Eiffel Tower.[29] But to

5 (*opposite*). *The Statue of Liberty, 1883*. V. Dargaud

6. Copy of the *Statue of Liberty*. Collas, 1885–9

have put the question to *Liberty*'s patrons of 1875 would have been to misunderstand both the situation and their methods. Liberty's triumph was only a tentative one; a reversal of events was always possible and indeed, as we have already noted, was soon to be attempted and on more than one occasion. A colossus of *Liberty* in Paris would, of course, have been hyperpotent politically. It might also, like the comte de Chambord's *fleur-de-lis*, have been just a little too much for the France of those years to bear. But the *temporary* erection of the statue in Paris – bringing to mind the great tradition in France of extravagant and outsized festival decoration and statuary – would make the point without peril; and from its prominent permanent site across the Atlantic it would continue to be felt. Like the depiction of sexual topics in the nineteenth century, this subject, though universal in appeal, was more readily confronted if transported to an exotic land or placed far away in time: America and 1776 fitted the bill very well. And indeed, not only would resistance be undermined, but the message would go deeper and reach a wider audience. To strengthen relations with America was a tradition reaching back to Louis XVI, who had sent Lafayette to help fight the natural enemy of France, Great Britain [7]. A century later, the game of international politics was not so very different. American feelings had been offended by Napoleon III's flirtation with the Confederacy and especially by his Mexican adventure, which he terminated only out of fear that the victorious republic would do so herself by force of arms. To smooth such ruffled feelings with a gift was an end to which all patriotic Frenchmen could subscribe.[30]

Liberty was thus more than an exile or expatriate; she was also an emissary. In fact – particularly when seen against the width of her support in France and the eventual assistance of the French state, which contributed a naval vessel for her shipment to New York in 1885 – *Liberty* appears as part of a diffuse but strong historical phenomenon: the contemporary tendency of France to project herself abroad – to export herself, as it were. There had been inter-

7. Indépendance des États-Unis.
L. Roger
after Duplessis-Bertaux, 1783

mittent colonialism throughout the mid-nineteenth century: Algeria during the July Monarchy; the Mexican adventure of Napoleon III; and then the enormous expansion after 1880 under Jules Ferry, in Tunisia and Indochina.[31] The increasingly ambitious International Expositions in Paris – 1855, 1867, 1878, 1889 – were specifically intended to spread the image of French industrial, scientific and cultural eminence throughout the world. France was the great missionary power of the time: in the last third of the century no less than three quarters of all the missionary priests of the Catholic Church were French. The religious emotion of those who remained at home went out, if not to heathen lands, to Rome and to the hopes of France fighting to restore temporal power to the Pope. Their prayer was: 'Save Rome and France in the name of the Sacred Heart.'

Liberty too formed part of this projection of France abroad. At one level Bartholdi's statue was what might be called a missionary icon of France – or at least of the political glory of her past and of her technical and cultural prowess in the present.[32] Americans appear to have sensed something of this, a pre-conscious perception that found expression in their initial mistrust, even hostility to the work. These misgivings were soon laid to rest for many by Emma Lazarus who, in her famous poem 'The New Colossus' (1883), falsely but gratifyingly interpreted the direction of *Liberty*'s gaze not as *away* from America but as America *welcoming* the new arrival, a turnabout of meaning (or at least a loss of the original sense) that was to be generally the statue's fate. In fact, even Emma Lazarus's interpretation, though remaining popular, was eventually to be displaced by something yet more innate to the United States, as we shall see.[33]

2. *Bartholdi*

Had Bartholdi, like most nineteenth-century sculptors, been consigned to the dust of history, one would not be obliged to apologize for his mediocrity as an artist. But one should not make too much of this. Bartholdi was far from being a sculptural hack, a sculptural everyman who stumbled into fame by grasping an improbable commission that happened to succeed. He was endowed, we shall find, with certain special gifts and talents. Moreover, he had certain traits of character – even idiosyncrasies – which take on significance in the context of the *Liberty* project.

Like so many of his time, Bartholdi was a passionate idealist – at least in public. A *Colmarien* from the heart of Alsace (whose ancestry went back, through Germany and Switzerland, to sixteenth-century Italy), he was an ardent patriot, especially during the Franco-Prussian War in which he was involved first as an overrun defender of Colmar, then as a starry-eyed aide-de-camp to Garibaldi in his attempt to lead a new French army against the Prussians, and finally as an Alsatian exile. Conceivably this bitter experience, especially the loss of his homeland, brought about his predilection for patriotic monuments after the war – in sharp contrast to his lack of any strong thematic commitment previously. He would not have been the only Frenchman converted by the experience of 1870–71; the idea of *revanche* was, after all, so powerful a force in France that half a century later it was to contribute to the causes of the Great War. Patriotic monuments became almost a 'vogue' after 1871.[1]

Although Bartholdi, after 1871, adopted a stance of fashionable political commitment, he remained, as an artist, firmly within the confines of his academic training in the studios of Etex, Soitoux and Ary Scheffer – the last, it may be noted, as ardent a republican politically as he was an idealizing sentimentalist artistically.[2] From the seventeenth century in France appropriateness of subject-matter had been at the center of academic doctrine. Bartholdi, who once declared that 'art is that sensation of the ideal imparted by the good and the beautiful',[3] would certainly have agreed with Poussin that in the 'grand manner . . . the first thing that, as the foundation of all others, is required, is that the subject-matter shall be grand, as are battles, heroic actions, and divine things . . . those who elect mean subjects take refuge in them because of the weakness of their talent.'[4] However, by the mid-nineteenth century, Realism had somewhat diluted the grand manner not only in subject-matter but in style.[5]

Bartholdi's fidelity to academic doctrine and his attraction toward large public monuments were concomitant. But the role of monument-maker, nowadays so unfashionable, needs some historical clarification.[6] Monuments, as understood here and as defined in the Introduction, belong to a kind of super-medium and though they usually take the form of a work of art they need not and do not always do so. Expressing the symbolic urge of a society, the monument has little inherent connection with the aesthetic volition of the artist. It conforms not so much with the inner vision of its creator, or of its private patron, as with the collective emotion and common denominator of taste prevalent in the society. But despite this theoretical distinction between a monument and a work of art there had traditionally been some congruence between them – a tradition maintained in the nineteenth century by such gifted sculptors as Rude and Carpeaux. After the mid-century, however, this began to break down, the sensitivities and needs of the public and those of the artist having by then diverged too widely. Rodin's *Balzac* provides the clearest illustration of this – of the public's hostility to a monument which took the form of a daring work of art. Yet it must be conceded that, great though the *Balzac* may be as a work of art, insofar as it was intended as a public monument its basic purpose was to cater to the crowd. However magnificent and truly monumental we may now think the result, Rodin had knowingly violated the 'contract' and his patrons reacted accordingly.

In this respect, as well as in others, Bartholdi was Rodin's opposite. By talent, temper and training Bartholdi was perfectly suited for the new specialist role of public monument maker. He did not produce, or perhaps even aspire to produce, museum art either for his own or any future age, yet we should not discount the relevance of his work, and that of those like him, to a public for whom monuments were still a prevalent concern. His very lack of a driving personal aesthetic allowed the academic compromise (in its variety of fashionable modes) to function untrammelled in his work as the universally palatable manner for a general practitioner of monuments. Bartholdi's career was not without frustrations and reverses, but they were never the result of controversial form or formal inadequacy. Perhaps it is a sad comment on his age, but Bartholdi was as perfectly equipped for success in building monuments for the late nineteenth century as Bernini was for Baroque Rome.

Thus Bartholdi's work, for the most part, bears little discernible stamp of formal originality, and resembles the output of a hundred other sculptors - and monument-makers - of his time. However, he did have one aesthetic passion - if it can be called that - a lust for the colossal. For Bartholdi this was more than just a means of achieving notoriety. Although the century's taste for the colossal in art, which Bartholdi so intensely shared, had its origins in the Neo-Classicism of the late eighteenth century, its awesome nature, its escape from the limitations of scale that confined ordinary sculpture, its suitability for 'sublime' natural settings, and its forbidding problems of execution all held great appeal for the Romantic sensibility that, in its late form, was another component of Bartholdi's artistic personality.[7]

In the fund-raising tract of 1885 that is such an important source for the history of *Liberty*, there is a special section on 'Colossal Sculpture'. The most telling passages are not Bartholdi's – that 'it ought to produce an emotion in the breast of the spectator' – but those of the more articulate writers he quotes. From Eugène Lesbazeilles's *Les Colosses anciens et modernes* of 1876 we read: 'It is within its scope when it represents power, majesty, infinity. It can lay claim to that class of effects which are produced in us by the heaving of the boundless sea, the bellowing of the wind, the rolling of the thunder.' Or from Charles Blanc, the celebrated art critic (founder of the *Gazette des Beaux Arts* and a family friend), writing in *Le Temps*: 'Colossal statuary calls for faculties of peculiar power. It is an art of an exceptional character, which presents considerable difficulties. The artist who approaches these difficulties enters a sombre temple, peopled with mysteries. He is brought face to face with struggles which few artists have experienced. No one can advise him, nothing can guide him except his instinct, his faith and his courage . . .' Although in fact the struggles of Manet or Rodin fall more truly within the sense of Blanc's words, he expressed perfectly Bartholdi's conception of his own career. Thus the sculptor's artistic creed superimposed two layers of ideology: the academic manner with its Poussinesque insistence on grand subject-matter, and the late-Romantic exaggeration of that ideal of grandeur in the swooning passion for the colossal.

In practice this combination involved nothing more than – quite literally – taking a stock academic figure and blowing it up to awesomely huge dimensions. The image could thus remain comfortingly familiar, while allowing us to indulge in the thrill of its monstrous scale. The experience – like that of the veiled erotic art of the academy – was gratifying to the Victorian, with his façade of impeccable respectability and his hidden lust. Little wonder that he built an army of colossi that earlier ages only dreamed of – perhaps in nightmares: the *Virgin* of Le Puy, the *Bavaria* in Munich, *Arminius* in the Teutoburger Wald and *Germania* on the Rhine

[37, 45–7]. *Liberty* was to be not only the largest, but the most successfully Neo-Classical in form, and, in her embodiment of a 'sublime' theme in a spectacular marine setting, the most Romantic as well.

Colossal scale was not something to which Bartholdi came late in his career. He had studied briefly with Etex, who had worked on the huge reliefs of the Arc de Triomphe de l'Étoile and brought Bartholdi close to the Napoleonic penchant for the colossal. Bartholdi's first success, a heroic bronze of General Rapp [8], 3.5 meters high on a pedestal of 4.2 meters, achieved notoriety

8. *General Rapp*. Bartholdi, 1855

for the young sculptor essentially because it was too large to fit in the exhibition hall of the Salon of 1855 and was consequently given a uniquely prominent exterior site, where it attracted the attention of critics, who not only took note of its 'colossal proportions' but managed to find praise for its form.[8] His career established, the following year Bartholdi accompanied Léon Gérôme, Bally, and Berchère – a group of orientalist painters – on a long trip to Egypt, a fashionable undertaking at the time. Bartholdi, very serious about the trip, not only made a number of remarkably good photographs (then becoming the rage), but took careful note of the great monuments that had drawn him on so long a journey [9]. And it was this voyage up the Nile that seems to have really brought out his latent attraction to the colossal. Classical sculpture, as he was well aware, had also produced notable colossi – the chryselephantine *Athena* [40] and *Zeus* of Phidias, each about forty feet in height (and exalted by Quatremère de Quincy in his *Jupiter Olympien*); or better still, for it was larger, the Colossus of Rhodes [63], as Bartholdi notes, 'the most celebrated colossal statue of antiquity'.[9] But these words existed solely in legend or in questionable reconstructions. The Egypt of Thebes and Abu Simbel remained for all to behold, and admire it Bartholdi most passionately did. Thirty years later (after an intermediate visit) he wrote:

'We are filled with profound emotion in the presence of these colossal witnesses, centuries old, of a past that to us is almost infinite, at whose feet so many generations, so many million existences, so many human glories, have rolled in the dust. These granite beings, in their imperturbable majesty, seem to be still listening to the most remote antiquity. Their kindly and impassible glance seems to ignore the present and to be fixed upon an unlimited future. These impressions are not the result simply of a beautiful spectacle, nor of the poetry of historic remembrances. They result from the character of the form and the expression of

9. Photograph by Bartholdi of the Colossi at Thebes, 1856

10. *The Lion of Belfort*. Bartholdi, 1875-80

the work in which the design itself expresses after a fashion in-finity.'[10]

Though his academic scruples prevented him from ever imitating Egyptian art directly – except for certain architectural references – its grandiose success in the colossal mode haunted him, and the dream of equalling it became a mainspring of his life. To a large extent this ambition can be said to have been fulfilled, for by far his most successful works – and they did bring him great fame – were the *Liberty* and the *Lion of Belfort* [10], a patriotic memorial to the town's heroic defenders of 1871 built into the cliffs below the fortress in the form of a twenty-two by eleven meter feline – a cross between Khafre's *Sphinx* at Gizeh and Thorvaldsen's *Lion of Lucerne*.[11]

The impetus for Bartholdi's two colossi came out of the war of 1870–71 and its aftermath. But already in the late years of the Second Empire, Bartholdi, encouraged, it seems, by the Empress Eugènie herself, had approached Ismail Pasha, ruler of Egypt, with a project during his visit to Paris in connection with the Universal Exposition of 1867. Ismail was the rage of Paris society, celebrated for his compelling combination of the oriental splendour of his entourage and his fully Europeanized personality and am-bitions to modernize Egypt (albeit with slave labor).[12] As Richard Wagner had perceived in Ludwig II of Bavaria a patron for his megalomaniac music, so in the extravagant character of Ismail, fully manifest at the 1867 fair (his 'Kiosk' there, incidentally, was purchased by Ludwig II for Schloss Linderhof!), Bartholdi saw the possibility of achieving a colossal project in the land of his dreams. Its location was to be at the entrance to the Suez Canal, nearing completion in 1867 when Bartholdi first proposed it [11]. In form a colossal *fellah*, many times lifesize and holding aloft a torch, the theme being 'Progress' or 'Egypt carrying the Light to Asia', it was to be the embodiment of Ismail's efforts at Europeani-zation and referred particularly to the great new canal itself.[13] It

11 (*left*). Sketch for Suez lighthouse.
Bartholdi, 1867

12. *La République*. Ary Scheffer, 1848

13. Lighthouse projects,
École des Beaux-Arts, 1852

was to serve as a lighthouse, thus recalling the Pharos of Alexandria. The sculptural mode of the project, however, may go back to a competition held by the École des Beaux-Arts in 1852 for an ideal lighthouse [13], several of the entries including bizarre figural components that recall the visionary architecture of the late eighteenth century, Lequeu's in particular.[14] And Bartholdi's design may also owe something to sketches made by his master, Ary Scheffer, in 1848, apparently in connection with the official competition in that year for an image of the new French Republic [12] and perhaps to other entries for the same competition which he may have known, such as that by his friend Gérôme and by Ange-Louis Janet-Lange [35]. But in the final analysis, visually the scheme depends most

strongly on the Colossus of Rhodes which, in traditional reconstructions, appears in a vast marine setting carrying a flame that
was thought to have served as a beacon – and which later was to be
a crucial source for *Liberty* [63].[15]

14 (*left*). Sketch for Suez Lighthouse.
Bartholdi, 1867–9

15A–D. Clay models
for Suez Lighthouse. Bartholdi, 1869

Bartholdi worked on the Suez project intermittently over the two succeeding years, experimenting with the movement of the figure in a number of clay maquettes and drawings [14, 15]. In 1869 he attended the festive opening ceremonies of the canal (for

which Verdi's *Aïda* was commissioned, although not completed
in time), taking the opportunity to solicit Ismail again. His response
was encouraging; he even involved himself in the scheme sufficiently
to suggest that the light be carried not in the hand but – native
style – atop the head. However, Ismail's interest was transient;
more pressing problems were soon to confront him.[16]

Later Bartholdi was to insist that his Suez project did indeed end
then and there, and that its manifest similarity to the *Statue of
Liberty* was a mere coincidence. He claimed that 'At that time
my Statue of Liberty did not exist, even in my imagination, and
the only resemblance between the drawing that I submitted to the
Khedive and the statue now in New York's beautiful harbor is
that both hold a light aloft. Now . . . how is a sculptor to make a
statue which is to serve the purpose of a lighthouse without making
it hold the light in the air? Would they have me make the figure . . .
hiding the light under its petticoat not to say under a bushel?'[17]

In his embarrassment at having this awkward subject suddenly
brought up in the course of a newspaper interview, Bartholdi
forgot that in the case of both the Suez *Progress* and the original
idea for the New York *Liberty* the lighthouse beacon was not
planned for the torch, but was to radiate from the forehead of the
figure; the torch was to be purely symbolic. He evaded the glaring
similarity of the two programs: colossal, robed, torch-bearing
females as lighthouses, sited at key points astride major waterways
of the world, symbolizing twin deities in the nineteenth-century
pantheon – Liberty and Progress – in both cases actively passing
their message from one continent to another. He claims at one
point to have 'never executed anything for the Khedive, except the
features of a female *fellah* . . .' and in another statement insists that
he did only 'a little sketch which has remained in his palace . . .'[18]
He fails to recall the series of maquettes done over a two-year period;
his encouragement by Eugènie; his trip to Egypt primarily to
obtain the commission; his stubborn insistence on pushing the

project despite the discouraging advice of Ferdinand de Lesseps, who, as builder of the canal, knew Ismail much better than the ambitious young sculptor did. Nor does he mention two drawings of 1869, now in the Bartholdi Museum, orientalizing and classicizing versions of a monumental building surmounted by a colossus

16. Project for Ismail Pasha. Bartholdi, 1869

of Ismail seated on a lion [16], presumably intended as a mausoleum for the ruler at his new city of Ismailia.[19]

The weakness of Bartholdi's attempt to play down his involvement with Egypt and to detach it from the *Liberty* project emerges when we discover what happened after Suez. We have seen that, according to Bartholdi's published account written in 1885, the seeds for *Liberty* were sown by Laboulaye as early as 1865.[20] But the first hints of the project in Bartholdi's private papers appear,

17. Sketch for the *Statue of Liberty*. Bartholdi, 1870

18. Terracotta model for *Liberty*. Bartholdi, *c.* 1870

19. Plaster model for *Liberty*. Bartholdi, 1871–5

we have noted, only in December 1869, and in the succeeding June in the form of oblique references to 'his American' and his 'dream of America', followed by his trip to America the next summer. It would therefore appear that upon returning from Egypt in the fall of 1869, Bartholdi sought to convert failure into success by re-directing his Egyptian project toward the old 'American' idea of Laboulaye, whose solicitations evidently continued throughout this period. (In the hope of achieving a colossus in *some* form, Bartholdi also projected, in 1869, a 25-35 meter equestrian *Ver-cingétorix* for Clermont-Ferrand, eventually executed at the end of the century at a mere six meters [60].)

The convergence of Suez and Glatigny can be seen in what appears to be the earliest model for *Liberty*, dated 1870 [17]. Its torch-lifting pose closely resembles the Egyptian project, but it is identifiable as *Liberty* by its classicizing physiognomy and costume (to become eventually a canonical tunic overlaid by a peplum) and by the broken fetters at its feet. In a larger and more finished version of this 1870 model now in the Museum of the City of New York (perhaps brought to the United States by Bartholdi in 1871) the radiant crown is already adumbrated, though Bartholdi appears to have been uncertain still about the attribute in *Liberty*'s left hand [18]. He substituted here a broken chain for the more traditional vase of the earlier model. The tablet was to appear only in the final version. Formally, too, this larger model falls between the strong twisting movement of the Egyptian projects and the extreme rigidity of the later, more mature model [19].[21]

All this might suggest that Bartholdi merely exploited the opportunity offered him by *Liberty*'s patrons, while they regarded him as little more than an instrument for realizing their ambitious propaganda. The relationship between them seems to have been symbiotic, Laboulaye's passion for liberty being complemented by Bartholdi's obsession with the colossal. Yet this is to over-simplify the matter. Bartholdi's words and deeds demonstrate that he too was a genuine partisan of liberty. His choice of the ardent republican

MORTS EN COMBATTANT
14 SEPT.^{re} 1870

20. *Monument funéraire*. Bartholdi, 1872

Ary Scheffer as a master perhaps revealed and surely reinforced his political leanings.[22] He was patriotically involved in the war, had been an associate of Garibaldi and was deeply wounded by the loss of his homeland. His sentiments found direct expression not only in the *Lion of Belfort* but also in other commemorative works, particularly the 'unknown soldier's' tomb at Colmar from which a hand reaches out to a sword beside it [20].[23] For Bartholdi liberty signified a cause as well as an opportunity. And there can be little doubt that it was political idealism – as well as artistic or professional ambition – that impelled him to devote himself for more than a decade to a project which often seemed all but hopeless and was to prove financially profitless.

But more deeply personal emotions were also involved. The loss of Alsace meant not only the expatriation of Bartholdi (he never returned to Colmar between 1872 and 1882), but the political bondage of his mother, who remained at home. As his father had died prematurely, his forceful mother played a dominant role in his life. A Protestant living in a Catholic community, she was something of a religious bigot who drove her other son, Charles, to madness and an early death by preventing him from marrying a local Jewess.[24] Bartholdi himself remained a bachelor until the age of 42 when, on his long visit to America in 1876, he met Jeanne-Émilie Baheux de Puysieux, a distant cousin of his friend, the prominent American artist John La Farge. She was impoverished and, as Bartholdi said, 'no brilliant match. There is neither wealth, nor beauty, nor society connections, nor musical talents.' Nor was there a solid enough Protestant background to satisfy Mme Bartholdi, though an obliging minister declared her to be a Unitarian, or at least 'a reasonable Protestant'. For fear of offending his mother's religious feelings, Bartholdi hesitated to marry her until he was almost obliged to do so in order to avoid a scandal which might have ruined the chances of his *Liberty* project.[25] She was to prove a good wife, selflessly devoted to him – 'a heart of gold' he confessed. But even after his marriage, Bartholdi's attachment to his mother remained his deepest emotion.

It is said that Jeanne-Emilie spent long hours posing for the figure of *Liberty*. But Bartholdi himself admitted that the face of the statue was his mother's [21].[26] And her hard dour features may, indeed, be recognized beneath the classicizing mask [22, 23]. For Bartholdi, the emotional core of meaning in his colossus was

21 (*left*). *Mme Bartholdi* (detail). Ary Scheffer

22. *Liberty*'s head during construction. New York, 1886

deeply personal – not America's achievement, not even the loss of his native Alsace, but the political degradation of his beloved mother. Thus, unlike other representations of liberty, Bartholdi's expresses not only triumph but embittered desire.

3. Liberty

24. 'Liberté'.
From J.-B. Huet: *Le trésor des artistes*, Paris 1810

The Goddess of Liberty was known as early as the Roman republic, which built a temple on the Aventine Hill to her in the third century B.C. But the ancient concept that she embodied was in origin personal rather than political. Liberty was simply the state of not being a slave. The Roman concept was embodied in art by a robed female holding a scepter (indicating sovereignty over herself), accompanied by a liberty-loving cat alongside a broken jug at her feet (symbol of confinement), and crowned by the Phrygian bonnet – the *pilleus libertatis* – bestowed upon slaves when granted freedom.[1] The image, seen already on republican coins, survived medieval interment and endured down to modern times,[2] being found in Cesare Ripa's great Renaissance iconographical compendium,[3] and as late as the nineteenth century [24] in J.-B. Huet's reduction of allegorical lore, *Le trésor des artistes* (1810).[4] In the various emblems and products of the French Revolution – including the many projects for liberty statues and celebrations – the form persisted.[5] On American coins the statutory emblem of liberty takes the traditional shape well into the nineteenth century, either fully enthroned or abbreviated (as on Roman coins) as a classical bust with an inscribed diadem and an occasional bonnet.[6] Liberty remains generally her classical self in other aspects of American imagery, both official and popular. Thomas Crawford's colossal bronze of 'Armed Liberty' on the dome of the Capitol in Washington (completed 1863) still carries the traditional iconographic apparatus.[7]

But even though it was possible in academic production to maintain the old image well into the nineteenth century, forces of change were in the making at all levels. For one thing, the traditional iconographic language was based largely on a system of symbolism whose roots lay in antiquity – the Phrygian bonnet being a good example. Even if maintained by the sheer weight of tradition, such allegory was no longer alive.[8] Its embalmed state in Huet's compendium is reflected not only in the chilly Neo-Classic illustrations, but in the detached tone of the text. The comments on liberty are typical: 'On prétend désigner par le sceptre l'empire absolu de la Liberté sur les hommes . . . on prétend également désigner par le Chat, l'instinct naturel de l'indépendance . . . [etc.]' The instability of the situation is well illustrated in American coinage: the Mint in 1859 – in a feat of unsurpassed iconographic hypocrisy – substituted for the bonneted classical profile, an Indian maiden (a traditional American emblem) with a feathered headdress inscribed 'Liberty', her new motto.

Liberty herself – and not just her trappings – had changed. In the nineteenth century liberty conveyed not so much freedom from actual slavery, which had been abolished in civilized countries, including the United States after 1865, but a much broader, more diffuse concept, involving liberties of many kinds, centering on the freedom of citizens from undue constraints on their life by legitimate rulers, or on their body politic by alien forces. Liberty was a fundamental prerequisite for democracy and therefore became a slogan of both French and American revolutionaries and their heirs.

It was not only a question of the decline of ancient allegorical devices and the rise of new political concepts. The first half of the nineteenth century saw a shift in representational style, not merely in the artists of the *avant garde* but of the old guard as well. In the second third of the century the reaction of such artists as Géricault and Delacroix in the teens and twenties against the strictures of Neo-Classicism had led to a kind of Baroque revival. The combination of realism and strongly expressive, dynamic forms penetrates sculpture in the work of Rude from the 1830s on, and his pupil Carpeaux in the 1850s and 1860s (and finally Rodin in the last third of the century). During the Second Empire, although dilute Neo-Classicism continued as part of the academic sculptor's stock-in-trade, the new style was widespread at the most common level of ambitious production – public monuments.[9]

All of this naturally affected the representation of 'liberty'. The traditional Ripaesque image would no longer do. Only one thing would remain unchanged: as with all such themes, the expression would be in allegorical form, as a personification. But both a new symbolism and a new manner of its presentation had to be found. During the period in question, we would expect such an iconographic vacuum to be filled in an eclectic manner. And indeed, we find, as in the case of other themes – such as the Republic – the operation of a syncretistic process, the fusion of borrowings from other stock allegorical imagery (not only Panofsky's 'pseudomorphosis', or the assumption of new meaning by old images, but a fusion of the results that we might call 'synthomorphosis').[10] Strongly influencing the resultant conformation of iconographic details was the new representational style and sensibility, which favored active, realistic attributes that would form natural relationships with the movement and expression of the figure, rather than being merely attached or a stage accompaniment.[11]

The transformation of liberty as an image can be seen in several monuments planned for the Place de la Bastille in Paris, scene of one of the events that sparked the Revolution in 1789 – the 'liberation' of the *ancien régime* fortress prison. Before events turned regicidal in 1793, it was planned to erect a column in honor of liberty on the site, to be surmounted by a statue of Louis XVI as a 'champion' of the people's liberty, with appropriate allegorical figures seated at the base.[12] Louis Philippe (disdaining Napoleon's mock-up, on the site, of a colossal elephant that still existed early in his reign)[13] may have been aware of this previous project when he ordered the still surviving – but seldom noticed – gargantuan column erected to celebrate the lesser revolution of July 1830 that had gratuitously brought him to power. The theme is still liberty, but it appears now neither as its 'defender' nor as the placid goddess of old. Rather the grandiose (and exquisitely wrought) column is surmounted by an activist 'genius' of liberty caught in full running stride – a travesty of Giovanni Bologna's *Mercury* – carrying aloft a flaming torch and a broken chain [25].[14]

The overt dynamism of the July Column *Liberty* was undoubtedly inspired by a better known work done just before it. In Delacroix's famous monument to the July Revolution – his *Le 28 Juillet, La Liberté guidant le peuple aux barricades*, painted in 1830 immediately following the uprising – liberty achieves a powerful impact mainly through a change in style [26]. It is recognizably the traditional goddess that dominates the great masterpiece, complete with Phrygian bonnet. But, with a rush like the genius of the column, she now strides powerfully forward carrying aloft the tricolor and bearing a flintlock, rather than standing meekly with a scepter. At her feet are heaped the corpses of the battle for freedom in place of a neatly set cat and broken jug. She is not nude but her clinging drapery falls, baring her great breasts. Not a

25 (*above*). *Genius of Liberty*. Dumont, *c*. 1840

26. *La Liberté guidant le peuple*. Delacroix, 1830

distant goddess of Olympus but of the earth and the people, she is the 'forte femme aux puissantes mamelles, à la voix rauque, aux durs appas' of Auguste Barbier's contemporary poem.[15]

Although it was clearly the power of Delacroix's Neo-Baroque brush that triumphed, he too was not without help from traditional sources. The victorious spirit of his *Liberty* is not fortuitous: it has been shown that her rushing form was inspired by ancient personifications of Victory.[16] Thus in both cases the process of 'pseudomorphosis' was crucial. In one instance an unimaginative academic sculptor simply borrowed a Renaissance Mercury intact, slightly recasting his role as messenger of the gods to one bearing a more contemporary message. In the other a great painter, whose genius lay so much in the power of authentic renewal of tradition, perceived in the dynamic movement of a Hellenistic type the means to re-animate a time-worn iconographic personage.

The ancient mold of Liberty had been shattered. When Bartholdi revived the theme a generation later there could be no going back to the pre-1830 form, particularly not in the case of a monument that was intended to carry a pointed message to a wide public. Yet the transformation of iconography in 1830 had not been without attendant problems. The barely visible Mercury-like figure atop the Bastille Column aroused little emotion. But Delacroix's work met quite another reaction. It suffered a long history that Bartholdi was certainly mostly aware of (if only through his teacher, the republican Ary Scheffer[17]), and it served him as both inspiration and warning.

Delacroix's *Liberty* had been so potent an image for its time that, unlike the aloof genius atop the Bastille Column, it was treated by the government as dangerously subversive – banished to an obscure Louvre corridor after being reluctantly purchased from the Salon of 1831; then returned for better safekeeping to the artist himself in 1839; and disallowed even from temporary exhibition in volatile Lyon in 1848. It only returned to the public eye after the unpredictable Napoleon III, being assured of its quality as a painting, allowed its exhibition in the Salon of 1855. His instinct was right: by then it proved to be politically impotent, essentially because its romantic style already was quite old-fashioned, dulling its revolutionary edge (General Franco, it will be remembered, now seeks to obtain Picasso's once inflammatory *Guernica* for Spain). Purchased by the state, Delacroix's painting hung in the Musée du Luxembourg until the moderate republicans in late 1874, on the eve of their tentative victory, felt quite secure in placing the image in the Louvre as a symbol of their emergent regime (as well as being, perhaps, another testing of public reaction to their mode of artistic propaganda in addition to Bartholdi's *Lafayette*).[18]

The ambiguity of Bartholdi's relationship to Delacroix's *Liberty* is evident. It was necessary to avoid truly revitalizing the powerful, revolutionary emotion the painting had originally provoked. Laboulaye, extremely cautious and sensitive to such questions – and who, let us remember, was an impressionable nineteen-year-old in 1830 – in an important fund-raising speech of 1876 alluded deprecatingly to Delacroix's *Liberty* as 'the one wearing a red bonnet on her head . . . who walks on corpses . . .' and felt that Bartholdi's more pacific image surpassed it.[19] One can appreciate his sentiment. Laboulaye was a retiring man of non-violent principles, who shunned violent tactics in politics: Bartholdi had replaced Delacroix's rifle with an engraved tablet, and the aggressively waved tricolor with a torch of Enlightenment. Laboulaye was also a pious man, and a bachelor: Delacroix's *Liberty* was a raucous, half-nude female, while Bartholdi's was decently covered up from neck to toe.[20]

Bringing Bartholdi improbably together with the great painter reveals, by contrast, the workings of the sculptor's imagination. Delacroix's image, in spite of its allegorical richness, effortlessly achieves an unsurpassed iconic density, a convincing sense of the rounded presence of a grand dramatic personage.[21] Bartholdi's creation is 'forced' [27]. Notwithstanding its scale, its relative formal simplicity, and its emphatic, if confined movement, the

27. *The Statue of Liberty*

statue yields a diffuse complex of iconographic intentions and allusions, giving the goddess a very complicated character indeed. What the observer seems finally to confront as he studies the figure is a kind of dramatic polymorph – just what one might have expected, in fact, from the combination of such extravagant ambition and such mediocre talent. If most of Bartholdi's sculptures – like those of his contemporaries – seem to represent bad actors, here an entire cast appears to inhabit a single figure.[22]

In pursuing this polymorphic spirit, *Liberty*'s iconography might be scrutinized from two points of view: as allusion to stock themes that she seems to recall; or according to the meanings of her individual attributes and aspects and the new totality they form. The latter, syncretistic approach is ultimately more revealing, but there are some obvious 'character' references that should first be observed. The primary allusion was to the figure of Faith as she appears, for example, in Ripa [28]; a helmeted, classical female in white, cradling in her left arm, together with the open book of the New Testament, the tablets of the Old (not unlike *Liberty*), and with the right hand raising aloft a heart with a flaming candle, symbol of the illuminative powers of Faith in dispelling ignorance and superstition. Bartholdi's transposition, characteristic of the influence of old religious forms on secular symbolism since the Revolution, was entirely fitting, Liberty being a central article of the creed of the left. However, other traditional personages are implicated as well – most meaningfully, perhaps, Truth [29], but also Doctrine, Eternal Felicity, Divinity, indeed, a host of figures sharing one or more attributes of Bartholdi's *Liberty* (especially the torch and nimbus). In moving beyond Faith, however, the focus tends to dissolve into an entanglement of references that form no sense of the 'Delacroixesque' *persona* we are in search of. Even Faith is a matter of intimation, not replication: strictly speaking, *Liberty*'s torch is not a heart with a flaming candle; her tablet is engraved with neither the Old nor the New Law; and so on. More important than her diffuse reincarnation of the old stock themes,

28. 'Fede Cattolica',
from C. Ripa: *Iconologia*,
Perugia 1766

29. 'Verità',
from C. Ripa: *Iconologia*,
Perugia 1766

Liberty was very much her own syncretistic self. Only by studying her features *as* her own – and not as mere reflections – do we gain a sense of her complex character.

With just-broken shackles still at her feet – like Courtaux's *La Grande Crucifiée* [4] – her grim face the stoic picture of suffering, Bartholdi's *Liberty* is a martyr. For her pains she has been elected for canonization. Unlike the image on Roman and American coins, her diadem does not bear the motto 'Liberty'. Rather, Bartholdi's goddess – a secular saint – emanates a nimbus of beatitude, as in the traditional iconography of Divine Wisdom, Eternal Felicity, Charity, Intelligence, and especially Faith.[23]

In *Liberty* the nimbus takes shape not as a solid halo but as the radiant antique crown. The device was originally borne by the Sun-God Helios (to be seen on ancient coins) and would logically have crowned the deity's grandest representation, the Colossus of Rhodes [63].[24] Although Bartholdi was particularly conscious of that construction – a colossus sited 'astride' a great harbor – he need not have gone back directly to it, for the radiant crown had known a long afterlife.

It was only natural that the divinely self-styled Roman emperors would appropriate it – as did Nero for his Colossus next to the Flavian Amphitheatre (the 'Colosseum') and Constantine for his portrait atop a column in the forum of Constantinople.[25] The motif re-emerges in the seventeenth century in an appropriate context: Bernini's equestrian statue of the first Christian emperor in the Vatican. However, for the nineteenth century the most influential post-antique version was undoubtedly atop Canova's massive *Faith* on the tomb of Clement XIII, also in St Peter's [30]. An important example of the Canovian type of powerful, almost masculine allegorical female, this ancestress of Bartholdi's work was widely published, appearing even in Lübke's universal sculptural history of 1863, and had an extensive progeny – for instance in Pio Fede's Niccolini monument of 1883 [31].[25A] By the mid-century the radiant crown had penetrated French State iconography: in

30. *Faith*, from the Clement XIII monument. Canova, 1787-92

31 (*right*). G. B. Niccolini monument, *Libertà*. P. Fede, 1883

Elias Robert's *La France couronnant Art et Science* of 1855 at the
Palais de l'Industrie [50] it replaces the crown of stars worn by
Robert's model, the figure of *La Patrie* at the Panthéon (1831-7) by
his master David d'Angers (in d'Angers' antecedent, in turn,
Cartelier's *Victory* of 1807 at the Louvre East Façade, the crown of
stars is suspended in mid-air). By the end of the Second Empire it
was extremely common, particularly in the state monuments of
Paris, occurring, for example, at the New Opera (1862-74) in figures
atop the façade and in numerous busts within the great staircase,
and in the spandrels of the vaults of the reading room of the Bibliothèque Nationale (1861-9) by Labrouste (whose atelier Bartholdi
had frequented).[26] But, despite the long pedigree of the motif
and its pervasiveness at the time, it is likely that Bartholdi was
aware that the seven canonical rays that his statue's head emanates
symbolized, in their original context, the sun's radiance to the
seven planets,[27] just as *Liberty* 'enlightens' the seven continents
and seas of the world. Nor was it entirely coincidental that Bartholdi's family emblem was a sunburst [32], going back to his

32. The 'Helios' in Bartholdi's study

paternal great-grandfather who took over his wife's prosperous family business, the 'Maison Sonntag'.[28] Thus the suffering visage of his mother appears to have duly received its aureole of beatification: for, we recall, it was she, in the guise of Liberty, who was the saint for Bartholdi.

But Bartholdi's martyr and secular saint, *Liberty*, is not only a passive exemplar of her faith; she is also an active protagonist of her idea. Reflecting the movement of the antique genius of the July Column and the flourished tricolor of Delacroix's painting, *Liberty* strides forward brandishing a flaming torch – another motif with both a long past and an active present. It shared with the nimbus the idea of radiance. Thus the two were often paired – as in Eternal Felicity, Divinity (two torches) and some versions of Faith; in some reconstructions of the Colossus of Rhodes; and in many public works of Bartholdi's day, as on the Opera façade and even at the Naturhistorisches Museum in Vienna [33] which carries Helios himself.[29]

33. *Helios*. J. Benk, 1876–8

Although this combination of motifs as such appears to form a tradition of its own that could well have influenced Bartholdi, let us closely consider the torch in isolation. Unlike the nimbus the possibilities of its meaning were ambiguous. Its activist nature could put it in the hands of such villainous themes as Calumny, Discord, and Slander (carrying twin torches like Divinity). Thus a torch-bearing figure could be interpreted as a dangerous firebrand as well as a Promethean hero, and the backers of *Liberty* were careful to make explicit which side they were on. In the words of Laboulaye, Bartholdi's figure 'will be the American Liberty who does not hold an incendiary torch, but a beacon which enlightens'.[30]

Apart from Faith, which we have already discussed, perhaps the most consequential example for *Liberty*, considering her role of 'enlightener', was Truth, who also holds an open book, related to the tablet. An intermediate position between Truth and Bartholdi's image can be found in a lithograph by Grandville and Daumier

of 1835 upholding freedom of the press, an acute issue of the day [34].[31] An exemplary instance of pseudomorphosis, the seemingly electrified torch is really the symbol of Truth in the guise of the Press, whose mission is to enlighten. In 1848 the torch passed into the hand of the French Republic in a painting which Ange-Louis Janet-Lange appears to have submitted as an entry in the official competition for an image of *La République*, though the painting was later titled *La France éclairant le monde* [35]. Here – rather significantly – the figure who holds the torch is enthroned above a plinth inscribed with the words *Liberté des cultes* and *Liberté de la presse*. In the following years the enlightening torch became a very widespread motif in sculpture, its dramatic

34. 'Soufflez, soufflez, vous ne l'éteindrez jamais'. Grandville and Daumier, 1835

35 (*opposite*). *La République* or *La France éclairant le monde*. Ange-Louis Janet-Lange, 1848

character fitting well the fashionable neo-Baroque style. Prominent instances abound – in the New Louvre with Jouffroy's *Commerce* and *Navigation* [36], or in Carpeaux's *La France portant la Lumière dans le Monde et protégeant l'Agriculture et les Sciences* of 1866 atop the Pavillon de Flore, not to mention the Opera façade sculptures already cited.[32]

Bartholdi's heroine had two strong arms, and he was not about to let either of them go unused. At first he placed in her left hand the ancient iconographic attribute of a broken vase [17], then

36. *Commerce* and *Navigation*.
F. Jouffroy, 1861–4

he substituted a broken chain [18], and finally an inscribed tablet –
JULY IV MDCCLXXVI – the necessary explicit reference to
American history and revolution, establishing her specifically as
American liberty [19].[33] Although shields and open books were
common sculptural devices for displaying inscriptions, stone
tablets were comparatively rare. When not in the hands of Moses
himself they generally embody a Mosaic reference, as in figures of
the Synagogue and Faith who usually display the Old Law on a
tablet. *Liberty*'s tablet – particularly the way it is borne forward –
is an unmistakable allusion not only to political events but to the
great Mosaic tradition. And, indeed, not only does she carry the
tablet of the patriarch but her radiant crown also may allude to
the 'rays of light' about his face after revelation. Thus she is, along
with everything else, a seer and a prophetess. Considered in this
way, her tablet bears not so much a remembrance as an implicit
commandment – Seek liberty! – and a prophecy: Liberty, as
achieved in America in 1776, shall spread throughout the world,
and most importantly, to France.

The ancient Goddess of Liberty had thus become not only a
reincarnation of such old themes as Faith and Truth, but assumed
in her own right a multiplicity of roles: martyr, secular saint,
prophetess and romantic heroine – all achieved largely by reference,
sometimes rather strained, to the traditional symbolic apparatus.
This complex, multiple program of meaning served the purposes
of the day, but was eventually to lose much of its integrity as the
historical conditions of its creation faded. The unwieldy iconographic machinery rusted, leaving the observer with a kind of
polymorphic iconographic blank that might be invested with a
variety of changing, up-dated symbols. However, on one level,
because of its ever increasing notoriety, the *total* configuration of
the statue became itself the symbol of liberty: the image of a single
work of sculpture took the place of the old idealist, allusive iconography Bartholdi had labored so hard to revive but which he
succeeded only in embalming.

The fate of Bartholdi's program included as well the explicit theme of the project – the still unexplained fact that his *Liberty* was conceived, in a mode that we might call gerundive allegory, as 'enlightening the world'. ('Enlightening', translated from 'éclairant', carries here the archaic sense of 'illumination' as well as the more specific 'instruction' it has become. An up-dated translation of the original French title might well be *Liberty Illuminating the World*.) The phrase has become a disposable appendage (the figure now being simply termed 'the Statue of Liberty'), but for Bartholdi and his patrons it was essential (and not only to camouflage the French 'imperialist' undertones that were discovered in Chapter 1). As in everything else about the statue the theme was not a particularly original one, neither as to its allegorical mode nor the topic of illuminant liberation. As one might have expected, the theme – ultimately stemming from St John's Neo-Platonic image of Christ as 'light of the world' (viii, 12) – goes back to the revolutionary period, when it was widespread in political thought. Although the philosophy of the Age of Enlightenment stressed that true liberty only came to those graced by the power of reason, in more poetic iconography Liberty herself possessed powers of enlightenment. As such the theme appears explicitly in a project that was surely one of the ancestors of Bartholdi's work, indeed, of his whole romance with America.

In 1791 Giuseppi Ceracchi, a Neo-Classical sculptor who had worked in England and in Paris, becoming preoccupied with revolutionary ideology through association with David (who in 1793 proposed to the Convention a colossus of 'Le Peuple Français' with *Lumière* inscribed on her forehead[34]), travelled to the United States and proposed to Congress a monument to Liberty. According to the sculptor's prospectus, it was to be a colossal group, 100 feet high, with scores of figures centering on the Goddess of Liberty represented 'descending in a car drawn by four horses, darting through a volume of clouds which conceals the summit of a rainbow . . . In her right hand she brandishes a flaming dart, which by dispelling the mists of error, illuminates the universe . . .' Needless to add, the project – which was to cost 'only $30,000' – met with no success and the sculptor returned to France, eventually to be guillotined for a conspiracy against Napoleon.[35]

In Bartholdi's time – particularly during the waning days of the Second Empire and shortly afterwards – the theme of 'enlightening' liberation was channeled primarily into political writings, being inadmissible in state sponsored art. However, in art one does find many examples of tamer illuminant imagery. Moreover, thematic composition turns strongly towards heavy gerundive allegory. The Salons of those years were replete with such subjects as, taking an example at random, Carrier-Belleuse's *Industry Bringing Peace and Light to the World* (1865). The situation is epitomized in two works already mentioned: Bartholdi's own *Egypt Passing the Light to Asia* – precursor to *Liberty Enlightening the World* – whose origin in 1867 suggests that Bartholdi took up (quite literally, like an Olympic torch-runner) Carpeaux's Louvre figure of 1866, *La France portant la Lumière dans le Monde*.

In political literature such imagery was generally very common in the wake of the *éclairés*. The theme of liberty as a prime agent of enlightenment is present throughout Laboulaye's writings. Yet, the history of the concept is even more specifically connected with Bartholdi's statue. For after the Declaration of Independence the United States became the embodiment of liberty for France; as Laboulaye wrote, Washington 'reconciled the world with liberty' (and certainly the American Revolution did contribute to the French event that followed). Such late-eighteenth-century statements as that of the French revolutionary figure, Cerutti – 'American independence is the tocsin of universal liberty'[36] – were bound to have an effect on later thinkers looking back. And in fact we find that the theme not just of illuminant liberty in general, but of America as liberty's light of the world pervades Laboulaye's writing. At one point, suggestively for our subject, it becomes quite explicit.

Laboulaye's most ambitious publication was his three-volume *History of the United States*, which took as long to complete as Bartholdi's statue (and is, in a way, its literary counterpart). Finished in 1866, it was begun in 1849 upon Laboulaye's receiving his chair at the Collège de France. Its avowed purpose – as we have noted – was to enlighten Frenchmen about the concrete possibilities of liberty in the American example; he wrote it in a state 'éclairé par l'exemple de l'Amérique . . .' In the prologue to the work, writing of the achievements of the founding fathers, Laboulaye relates the story of Franklin – together with Washington, his American hero – at the last session of the triumphant Constitutional Convention. During the whole convocation Franklin had been thinking of the image of the rising sun behind the president's chair and 'was incapable of deciding if the sun was rising or setting.' He then exuberantly exclaimed, 'Now, at the end, I am happy to see that it is clearly a rising sun and not a sun becoming extinct.' 'Franklin was right,' concluded Laboulaye, 'it was the dawn of a new world . . . it was liberty that rose on the other side of the Atlantic to enlighten . . . the universe.'[37]

In his history Laboulaye's poetic phrasing of the political sentiment was essentially metaphorical. But when the notion was directed to the theme of a monument actually to be built, it became more than a poetic phrase: it was truly a visionary image that captured the fancy of Bartholdi and his patrons. In their imagination the figure loomed so large and bright it could be seen across the Atlantic.[38]

This is latent already in the first public prospectus, published in 1875: 'On the threshold of this vast continent, full of a new life, where all the ships of the universe arrive, she will rise from the bosom of the waves . . . at night a luminous halo extending from her forehead will shine afar on the immense sea.'[39] A year later the refrain of Gounod's fund-raising 'Liberty Cantata' (performed at the Opera in Paris) proclaims: 'Je porte au loin dans la nuit sombre, / Quand tous mes feux sont allumés, / Mes rayons au vaisseau qui sombre, / Et ma lumière aux opprimés.' But curiously, the visionary notion was laid bare most unequivocally in the acceptance speech of President Grover Cleveland at the unveiling ceremony in 1886:

'We will not forget that *Liberty* has made here her home, nor shall her chosen altar be neglected. Willing votaries will constantly keep alive its fires and these shall gleam upon the shores of our sister Republic in the East. Reflected thence and joined with answering rays, a stream of light shall pierce the darkness of ignorance and man's oppression until Liberty enlightens the world.'[40]

Laboulaye himself could not have put it any better.

4. The Colossal Vision

The visionary aspirations of Bartholdi and Laboulaye owed much to revolutionary and Romantic ideas. But they were just as deeply rooted in the great tradition of visionary art in France – a tradition, it may even be said, to overshadow that of every other western nation. It was in France that the first truly successful visionary architecture of the West was achieved – the Gothic cathedral, which seems even more immense than it is, the very image of an aspiration to the infinite. It was later in France that perhaps the most ambitious visionary – as opposed to merely large – monument of the post-medieval age was built: the palace and gardens of Versailles. France is the country from which sprang the Utopian architecture of the later eighteenth century – the dreams of Boullée and Ledoux – and where the most influential visionary architect of modern times – Le Corbusier – had, if not his birth, his spiritual home. And it is Paris that is dominated by the Eiffel Tower.

The glories of the French visionary tradition were almost exclusively architectural and abstract, as opposed to figurative and sculptural. Despite their myriad carvings the dominant impression of the Gothic cathedrals is an architectural one, and of the later visionary achievements this is perhaps even truer. Indeed, this strain attains its purest expression in the projects of Boullée and Ledoux.[1] Although the Napoleonic period that followed tended towards sculptural enrichment, it is still an architectural impression that dominates the Vendôme Column or the Arc de Triomphe de l'Étoile. It was characteristic of France that the colossal sculptural monuments of the time were all abortive (or short-lived). David's fervent proposal, already mentioned, at the height of the Revolution, for a Herculean colossus resting on a club and carrying in one hand *Liberty* and *Equality* ('prêtes à parcourir le monde'), its body inscribed with other revolutionary mottoes, was executed only in plaster, at half the intended scale of 50 ft. After many difficulties the single colossal bronze figure of the period, the *General Desaix* by Dejoux – only fifteen feet high at that – was cast in 1807, but after the Restoration was soon melted down. The forty-foot elephant, carrying a tower in the manner of the ancients, planned for the Place de la Bastille from 1808 on was achieved only in lath and plaster. Although the idea was kept alive for several decades, it was vilified by Quatremère de Quincy – aesthetic arbiter of the early century, who in his *Jupiter Olympien* (1814) had advocated colossal statuary in the mode of Phidias – as 'Le monstreux colosse'; and the mock-up gradually rotted away, finally to be torn down in 1848 after having been immortalized by Hugo in *Les Misérables* ('la nuit, sur le ciel étoilé, une silhouette surprenante et terrible . . . c'était sombre, énigmatique et immense . . .').[2] Even under the strain of megalomaniac leaders, it seems, French sensibility avoided colossal statuary. The single permanent visionary monument of modern Paris (the quarter-scale copy of the *Statue of Liberty* having been deposited on an obscure island in the Seine) was to be the Eiffel Tower, so radically abstract a work that it shocked the guardians of French tradition [6, 73].

Thus while the great French visionary tradition undoubtedly influenced and possibly inspired Bartholdi, it provided him with very few models for a colossus. Aside from theory and such fanciful projects as Lequeu's fantasies, David's *Le Peuple Français* or the 1852 lighthouse competition [13], there were, it seems, only two notable French examples of colossal statuary that affected Bartholdi: the sixteen-meter *Virgin* of Le Puy (1857–60) that stands remotely isolated on a volcanic eminence over the picturesque provincial

37. *Notre-Dame de France.*
J. Bonnasieux, 1857-60

capital [37]; and, smaller and even farther from Paris, the nine-meter *Virgin* over the façade tower (forty-five meters) of Notre-Dame-de-la-Garde (1854–64) built on a steep hill overlooking the harbor of Marseilles. Bartholdi mentions (and illustrates) the Le Puy *Virgin* in his *Liberty* apologia; and he must have known the Marseilles figure since it was going up when he was there in 1859. These two giant *Virgins* appeared at an early point in Bartholdi's career (although *after* his heroic Colmar statues and his visit to Egypt) and may well have reinforced his growing predilection for the colossal.[3] Moreover, they dominate picturesque land and marine settings – as Bartholdi's own colossal works were to do. But even so, their influence and that of his other French sources were probably minor. The principal impetus and the models for his involvement with the colossus (as distinct from the colossal) came, as already noted, from elsewhere, from the tradition originating in antiquity and continuing in practice in modern Europe most impressively outside France.

We have referred to Bartholdi's visits to Egypt and, obsessed though he clearly was by the colossi on the Nile, his imagination was also haunted by the phantoms of Graeco-Roman colossal statuary which his academic training had taught him to emulate. There were the famous chryselephantine masterpieces of Phidias, the colossi of Olympia and the Acropolis (and *Liberty* is not to be understood without reference to the *Athena Parthenos* [40] and *Promachos* of which copies, especially of the former, adorned many projects of the period, e.g. the Parliament in Vienna[4]). Then, too, *Liberty* was associated in everyone's mind with the Colossus of Rhodes – probably her single most important source – whose imagined height Bartholdi exulted in having surpassed and which was described by Laboulaye as a 'child's toy' in comparison.[5] (It was later declared a morally inferior 'brazen giant of Greek fame' by Emma Lazarus.) But the most extravagant project of antique legend – and one from which Bartholdi may have taken a lesson in the politics of patronage – was the proposal of Deinocrates, who flattered Alexander the Great with the idea of carving the entire Mount Athos into a figure of the conqueror, one hand carrying a city, the other holding a shell in which the waters of the mountain would collect and spill into the sea.[6]

Free-standing statues that had been so popular in antiquity were rare in the Middle Ages, nor were any true colossi erected. Some huge figures were made – such as the four-meter Kings in the gallery of the façade of Reims cathedral, though they do not appear to be 'colossal' in their place far above the observer in a gigantic architectural framework. Nor was the five-and-a-half-meter *St Christopher* of 1331 on the façade of Gemona Cathedral a true colossus: the figure is merely natural scale, for St Christopher *was* a giant.[7]

It was the Italian Renaissance, as Bartholdi was aware, which first revived the colossal art of antiquity.[8] The process of revival – begun in Florence – was a typical historical mixture of coincidence and conscious intent. Carrying through a medieval cycle, the fourteenth century Florentines planned figures of prophets to stand over the upper parts of their new cathedral. One of these was executed by Donatello, an eighteen-foot *Joshua* completed in 1419 (and eventually lost). Later in the century a companion piece was commissioned from Agostino di Duccio. It was the uncompleted marble block of this figure – which had only barely been begun – that was inherited by Michelangelo and carved into the *David* in 1501-4. Like the *Joshua*, the huge figure was first intended to stand high up on the cathedral. It would have thus remained essentially in the medieval mode exemplified by the Kings of Reims – a pseudo-colossus – had the Florentines (Michelangelo among them) not decided to keep it on the ground as a civic symbol, transforming it thereby into the first true colossus since antiquity.[9]

The *David* was not the only colossal project of Michelangelo, nor was Michelangelo the only Renaissance sculptor concerned with colossal statuary.[10] With its adulation of Man, it was only natural that the colossal – or at least the heroically scaled – re-creation of the human form should be emulated in Renaissance art.[11] But Bartholdi explicitly mentions only two examples, both from the late Renaissance: Giovanni da Bologna's grotesque *Appenino* of 1580 and the truly colossal *S. Carlo Borromeo* – twenty-three meters high on a twelve-meter pedestal – at Arona on Lago Maggiore of the early seventeenth century [38]. It is revealing that although Bartholdi was influenced by the technique of the *S. Carlo Borromeo*, which he visited on returning from Suez, he disparaged it, writing that it cannot be 'properly included

38. *S. Carlo Borromeo.*
G. B. Crespi, 1610-96

under the heading of colossal art. It is an ordinary [portrait] statue enlarged . . .'[12]

The Renaissance colossi, with a few exceptions, are restricted in scale, being, like the *David*, marginally rather than truly colossal in size (which is to say, one could still faintly imagine them engaging in relations with normal humans).[13] Although the Renaissance glorified man, it was controlled – if decreasingly – by humanist thought, which was hostile to the radically superhuman, an aspect of the antique inheritance that clashed with the vision of man as the 'measure of all things'. (Even Michelangelo, who at Carrara had toyed with the Deinocratian notion of carving a whole mountain into a statue, spurned with silence and then with a famous comic letter the proposal of Clement VII to erect a forty-braccia [*c.* 23 meters] colossus near S. Lorenzo in Florence.)[14]

The real post-antique revival of the colossus on the grand scale dates from a more violently emotional and, at the same time, more archaeologically 'correct' period, that of the Romantic Neo-Classicism of the late eighteenth century. If in France the most impressive ideas in this realm were visionary architectural projects (against which Quatremère de Quincy's Phidian revival seems rather pedestrian), colossal sculpture became a principal mode of expression in surrounding countries.

In Italy the great Neo-Classical sculptor Canova, possibly influenced by Quatremère de Quincy, not only resurrected the heavily draped, massive female type of fifth-century Greece, but in his projected figure of Religion [39], which was to be some eight meters tall (extraordinary for a marble statue) he revived the scale as well of the major example of the mode, the *Athena Parthenos* of Phidias [40]. Dating from 1814, it strangely anticipated the history of *Liberty*. The *Religion* was to have been an outright gift from Canova to the basilica of St Peter's, in honor of the 'Faith of his Fathers' and the Pope. But, for reasons not entirely clear, the canons of the Holy See obstructed the gift, not even allowing Canova to erect it in the Pantheon as an alternative (later, we shall

39. *Religion.* Canova, 1814

40 (*right*) *Athena Parthenos.*
Roman marble copy.

see, *Liberty* found a similarly cool reception from the Americans).
Rejected by the Roman clergy, the work was nevertheless eventually executed by the disappointed sculptor for an English tomb at
one-half scale. Just as Bartholdi's Suez project was transposed into
the New York colossus, so Canova transformed his figure into
Protestant Religion by deftly removing the awkwardly set papal
tiara and stole. And just as Bartholdi himself realized his Suez
project in New York, so a mid-century follower of Canova executed

his Roman one at full-scale at Genoa in a nine-meter figure of Faith that Bartholdi, well-traveled in north Italy, might easily have known [41].[15]

Equally characteristic of the trend was the extraordinary project of 1799 of Canova's English contemporary, John Flaxman, for a statue of Britannia ('by Divine Providence Triumphant') no less than 230 feet in height [42]. It was to be erected on the summit of Greenwich (by the observatory) where it would be visible to travellers 'from Europe, Asia, and Africa' on their way to London along the Thames or on the Dover road, as a national memorial to the naval victory over the French at the Battle of the Nile. The idea

41 (*left*). *Faith*. S. Varni, *c*. 1850

42. *Britannia*. J. Flaxman, 1799

may represent a response to David's *Le Peuple Français* – also to have been a colossus commemorating national triumph. But in Flaxman's publication of the project, the conception is frankly derivative of the Phidian *Athena* and the Colossus of Rhodes in form, scale and site respectively (although its rigidity more truly resembles such early Classic sculpture as the Olympian *Athena*). And suggestively foreshadowing the *Statue of Liberty*'s visionary terrestrial prominence and directionality, Flaxman emphasizes that, 'as Greenwich Hill is the place from whence the longitude is taken, the Monument would, like the first Mile-Stone in the city of Rome, be the point from which the world would be measured'.[16] Flaxman's fantastic idea – the megalomaniac scale of which may have been partly inspired by 'The Monument', the giant 202 foot column commemorating the Great Fire of London in 1666 – although of course never taken quite seriously, did exert some hold over the minds of English artists, for as late as 1839 a similar figure of Britannia, reduced in size to a mere 120 feet, appears in a project for the Nelson memorial in Trafalgar Square. The idea thereafter was lost to England for, with the exception of the Wyatts' thirty-foot equestrian Wellington Monument at Constitution Hill of 1838–46, none of the great English monuments of the mid-century – the Wellington Monument in St Paul's, the Nelson Memorial, the Albert Memorial in Hyde Park – was formed with such bold austerity.[17]

It was in Germany – finding a place in the European sun as its political fortunes rose through the century – that the colossus was first and most numerously realized in the period. The impulse was not altogether new to Germany. The way had been prepared by certain plates in Fischer von Erlach's *Entwurf einer historischen Architektur* (1721) and by Guernieri's *Hercules* in Kassel [43]. Then in 1796 Friedrich Gilly proposed an extraordinary (and ultimately influential) architectural monument to Frederick the Great, in the form of a huge Doric temple on a massive substructure. A generation later the desire to commemorate the great national figure was

43. *Hercules*. G. F. Guernieri and J. J. Anthoni, 1701–18

taken up by his descendant, Friedrich Wilhelm IV, himself an ambitious architectural dilettante. As part of his projects to embellish Potsdam, as early as the 1820s he proposed to represent his ancestor as a seated, nude, ancient colossus (on a scale suitable for marriage with Flaxman's *Britannia*) crowned with a laurel wreath, a spear in one hand, set over a huge Neo-Classic, pediment-less Doric substructure[18] – a project that, with Flaxman's, provides a noble ancestry for Bartholdi's *Liberty* [44].

44. *Monument to Frederick the Great.*
Friedrich Wilhelm IV, *c.* 1820-30

The first of the Teutonic colossi to be actually erected was Schwanthaler's *Bavaria* in Munich [45], begun in 1837 and completed in 1848 (but only first exhibited in 1850 after the sculptor's death).[19] Set over a nine-meter pedestal, the eighteen-meter high, heavily robed, rather dumpy wreath-lifting figure is accompanied by a lion, possibly going back to Flaxman's project. (In-

45. *Bavaria*. L. Schwanthaler, 1837–48

terestingly, a full-scale copy of *Bavaria*'s head was on exhibit together with reproductions of Abu Simbel at London's great Crystal Palace, and remained on exhibition after the construction was moved to its permanent site at Sydenham in 1852.)

Because of its primacy in realization and its site in a European capital, *Bavaria* was, and remains, the most famous of the nineteenth-century precursors to Bartholdi's *Liberty*, a primacy which he acknowledged. However, it was another, and even larger German colossus mentioned by Bartholdi that may have had a deeper influence on him, a work which in many ways provides an earlier analogue to *Liberty*. A columnar monument to the barbarian hero Arminius (Hermann), who had successfully resisted the eastward push of the Romans (and who, between 1750 and 1850, was celebrated in no less than 200 plays and other productions) had been mooted as early as 1782. At the end of the Napoleonic wars – for Germany, the 'Freiheitskriege' – the idea was revived by Karl Friedrich Schinkel, in the form of a spectacular project for an immense battle group, on the visionary scale and in the Romantic style of Boullée's grandest architectural conceptions, transposed into the medium of colossal statuary. Although Schinkel was still promoting his projects for a *Hermannsdenkmal* in 1839, it was – characteristically – a lesser artist who, by his willingness to devote thirty-nine years to the project, was finally able to realize it. In 1819, still in his youth, the sculptor Ernst von Bandel fixed on the idea. A dominant motivation was the explicit desire to call the Germans to unity. By 1835 his final project was settled (to be financed by the solicitations of 'Hermannsverein' chapters scattered over Germany and in other Francophobic lands as well), a fifty-three-meter monument to be built in the Teutoburger Wald near Detmold in Westphalia [46]. Standing atop an enormous (twenty-seven meters high) and curious neo-Medieval pedestal that bears symbolic allusions similar to those of the unexecuted projects for *Liberty*'s base (which we shall examine in due course), the rudely fierce, Wagnerian protagonist energetically lifts his sword to the sky in a movement that closely resembles the upward thrust of *Liberty*'s torch, even in the way the arm turns in grasping the handle of the instrument. The similarities to Bartholdi's project – the political motivation, the symbolism of the base, the outline of the figure, the Romantic setting, even the technique of repoussé

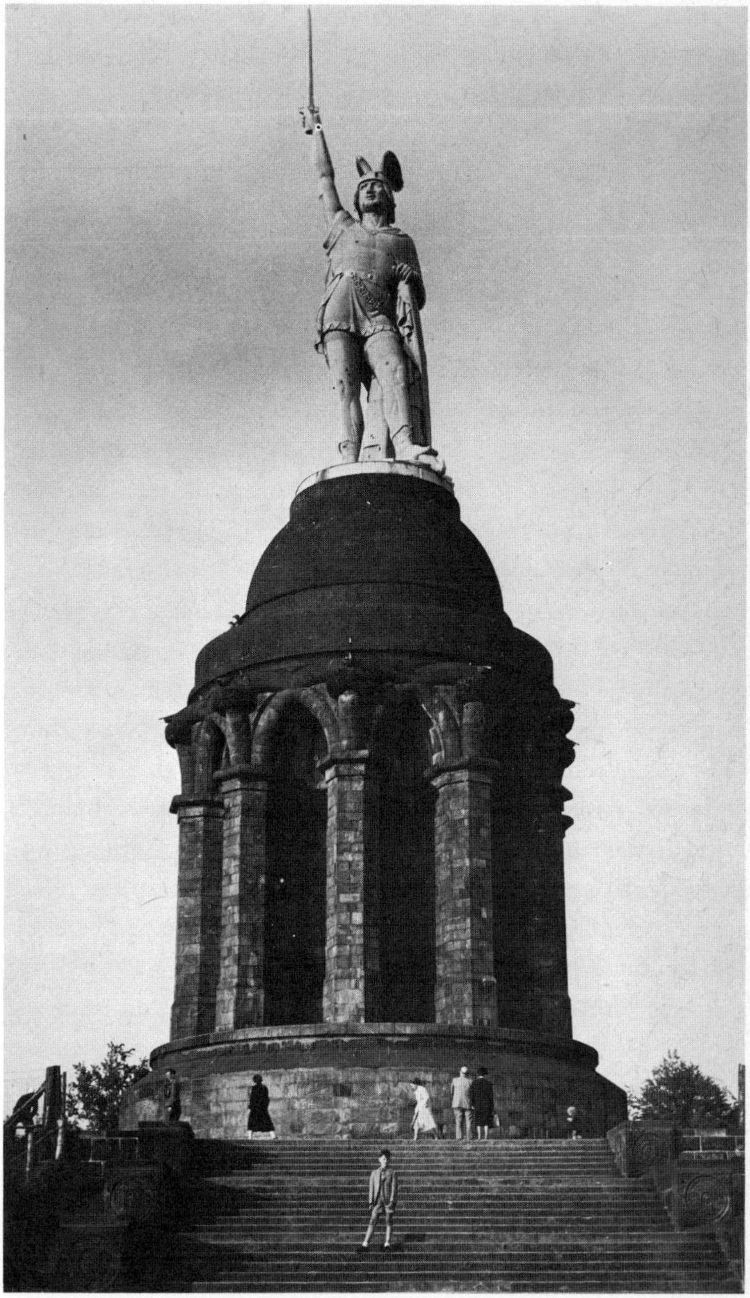

46. *Arminius*. E. von Bandel, 1819–75

copper on an iron framework – were undoubtedly more than coincidental. Although the socle was completed by 1846, work on the figure continued down to its dedication in 1875 – the year *Liberty* became public.

During this long period of execution the political situation had changed: not only had Germany achieved unity and power, it had devastatingly defeated a formerly proud France. It was not only the iconography and form of the Hermannsdenkmal (as the Germans call it) that would have affected Bartholdi: its inscriptions were as provocative as the Ems Dispatch, declaring, 'Nur weil deutsches Volk verwelscht und durch Uneinigkeit machtlos geworden war, konnte Napoleon Bonaparte, Kaiser der Franzosen, mit Hilfe Deutscher Deutsche unterjochen; da endlich 1814 scharten sich um das von Preussen erhobene Schwert alle deutschen Stämme, ihrem Vaterland aus Schmach die Freiheit erkämpfend' and, on the other tablet, 'Am 17. Juli 1870 erklärte Frankreichs Kaiser, Louis Napoleon, Preussen Krieg, da erstunden alle Volksstämme Deutschlands und züchtigen von August 1870 bis Januar 1871 immer siegreich französischen Übermut . . .' ('It was only because the Germans had become so frenchified and so weakened through disunity that Napoleon Bonaparte, Emperor of the French, was able to conquer them, subduing Germans with the help of Germans. Finally in 1814 all the German races rallied round the sword raised by the Prussians in order to win by battle the freedom of the fatherland from humiliation.' 'On 17 July 1870 the Emperor of the French, Louis Napoleon, declared war on Prussia. Thus all the German peoples rose up and, between August 1870 and January 1871, ever victorious, chastised French arrogance.')[20]

Less than a year after the message of von Bandel's statue had been twisted to express the new European balance of power, the Kaiser laid the cornerstone to a militaristic monument designed to flaunt his humiliation of France: the *Germania* – a ten-meter figure not entirely unlike *Liberty* in its dynamic form – set up near

47. *Germania*. J. Schilling,
1876–83

Rüdesheim and directing its gaze westward towards France from a
hilltop overlooking the Rhine [47].[21]

The Frenchmen of the 1870s needed no reminder of their defeat
by England in 1814 and Germany in 1871. Their decline was not
only one of military prowess and political integrity. They had been
left far behind, by the early nineteenth century, in such critical
matters as the production of coal and iron and the building of heavy
machinery and railroads. Paris had its New Opera, its New Louvre
and its great urban renewal by Haussmann – but no energy was
left for pure, non-functional monuments of equivalent ambition.[22]

The age of material triumph substituted sheer size for formal grandeur. In contemporary publications of the colossi it is their immense size and the dazzling techniques of their execution that always seize the imagination.[23] When France – whose popular motto already under Louis Philippe had been *enrichissez-vous* ('get rich') – finally began actually to catch up materially with her rivals (beginning in the mid-1870s), it would not be long before the colossus, the materialist monument *par excellence*, appeared – if only for temporary exhibition.[24]

Bartholdi's *Liberty* marked the joyous entrance of France into the mainstream of the industrial age and the materialist aesthetic that was to find its definitive expression a decade later, when the economic star of France had truly risen, in what was to become the most famous French monument of all, the Eiffel Tower, proudly put up for the Fair of 1889. But already with *Liberty* the materialist aesthetic went beyond her sheer size, for the notion of 'enlighten-ment' was expressed quite literally with one of the great inventions of the age, electric light. And, at the same time, this made her a functioning lighthouse, also a matter of deep satisfaction to the utilitarian sensibility.[25] The sheer material glory of *Liberty* was certainly one of the reasons why she was financially backed so enthusiastically by the French.

Thus, Romantic Neo-Classicism, nationalistic aspirations and pride, and culturally pervasive materialism combined to make the nineteenth century a great period of the outsized monument and especially the colossus. As the mid-century became the late century the momentum of colossus building increased, topping out a thickening forest of monuments of more ordinary scale that almost threatened to choke the city squares and picturesque sites of Europe – so that at one point in Paris a moratorium on monuments was proposed. (Even in America, where ambitious statuary me-morials were scarcer, there was the unrivalled 555-foot Washington Monument, 1848–84.) The *Statue of Liberty* marked the culmina-tion of the movement. Within a decade after its completion in 1886

48A. Kaiser Wilhelm Monument.
B. Schmitz, 1897

48B. *Völkerschlachtdenkmal.*
B. Schmitz, 1898–1913

49. *The Republic*. D. C. French, 1893

the colossal mode turned bitter, shifting from a still innocent pomposity to a bombastic harshness, most sharply in the nightmarish German monuments of Bruno Schmitz, whose Bismarckian style achieves full brutality in 1897 at the Kaiserdenkmal am Deutschen Eck at Koblenz [48A] and its apotheosis a few years later at the terrifying Völkerschlachtdenkmal at Leipzig [48B], which casts its long shadow down to the Germany of the 1930s.[26] This late-nineteenth-century brutalism can be seen as early as the Piranesian distortions of scale in the main façade of the Palace of Justice in Brussels (1866–83).[27] It traversed the Alps to the Victor Emmanuel Monument in Rome (1885–1911), and even crossed the Atlantic to appear in the chillingly rigid and severe sixty-five-foot plaster figure of *The Republic* erected by Daniel Chester French for the Chicago Fair of 1893 – against which Bartholdi's colossus, for all its inadequacies, appears the embodiment of elegance and grace [49].[28]

5. The Site

50. *La France couronnant Art et Science*, E. Robert, 1855

The robust female figure, striding forward or standing tensely erect, holding aloft a symbolic instrument – usually a torch or banner – with a generally dynamic treatment of drapery and a contained passion in her thick classicizing physiognomy, is a familiar stock personage in academic art, particularly in the mid- and late-nineteenth century. It was eminently adaptable to stand either alone or within a monumental scheme. We have already, in fact, seen prominent examples of the type in Canova's *Religion* and, a generation later, Delacroix's *Liberty*. She reappears in the projects for a national figure of the Republic of 1848 which included a contribution from Bartholdi's teacher Ary Scheffer [12].[1] The triumphal entrance to the Palais de l'Industrie of the first Paris International Exposition – the year 1855 when Bartholdi's *General Rapp* scored his first Salon success – was topped by a super-Canovian figure of *France* [50] holding aloft two wreaths (a slight variant of the type in question) and whose massive stature, pose, physiognomy, drapery and radiant crown unmistakably point to Bartholdi's less stolid figure of twenty years afterwards. But as strongly influential as these specific examples suggest themselves to have been, it is impossible to pin down *Liberty*'s model exactly. Particularly as we move towards 1870 the frequency of the general type increases. It abounds in the Second Empire, appearing in the New Opera, where candelabra-figures populate the grand staircase, and in the New Louvre,[2] and even on the façade of the Gare du Nord.

The pervasiveness of the type can perhaps be best suggested by two examples outside sculpture. One of the most popular paintings in the 1859 Salon was Charles-Victor-Eugène Lefebvre's *Truth* [51] – a sensual nude clutching a banner in her left hand and her right arm thrusting aloft a seemingly electrified version of her traditional torch.[3] The similarity of this figure to *Liberty* is not only evidence of the latter's iconographic pseudomorphosis (the borrowed torch), but *Truth* reveals what the nineteenth-century eye would undoubtedly have imagined beneath *Liberty*'s thick antique drapery – a characteristic academic nude of the later nineteenth century, large boned, massively curved, substantial and severe, with few traces of delicate feminity, altogether a fit companion for the iron men who dominated the age. A generation later, on the other side of the Atlantic, we find Mrs Cornelius Vanderbilt, photographed as she wished in the costume 'The Electric Light' she wore at a famous fancy dress ball of 1883 that was given by, and socially established, her sister-in-law Mrs W. K. Vanderbilt [52].[4] Although the *Liberty* project was well known to New Yorkers by 1883,[5] it is impossible to tell if Mrs Vanderbilt was mimicking Bartholdi's project, or merely taking up a modish posture.

The *Statue of Liberty* embodied an unsurpassably common pose, but its particulars and drapery details – like its thematic attributes – were thoughtfully devised. Before considering these details, however, it is necessary to explore the relationship between the site, the observer and the statue from which the most interesting aspects of the sculptural form derive. A marine setting was hardly an original notion. As we have already seen, colossi had from the earliest times often stood or been intended to stand either in or near water. This tradition seems to have influenced the transformation of the lighthouse into a colossus as in the 1852 lighthouse competition (the Colossus of Rhodes had also been a kind of lighthouse). In Bartholdi's work this combination appears first in the

51. *Truth.* C.-V.-E. Lefebvre, 1859

52. Mrs Cornelius Vanderbilt
as 'The Electric Light', 1883

1867-9 Suez project. The extension of this idea to New York harbor was, nevertheless, an impressive creative act. Bartholdi perceived not only the romance and grandeur of the setting but the significance of the site as the main gateway to the New World

53. New York Harbor *c.* 1886–90

54 (*left*). Immigrants' shipboard view of *Liberty*. 1887

[53]. He must have appreciated how a statue in New York harbor would burn into the memory of all the travellers and immigrants who would be greeted by it after weeks on the Atlantic [54].

The statue was clearly not intended to be inspected critically from every point of view – the back is residual and awkward – but through a long arc (somewhat less than a half circle) running from the entrance to the harbor (the Verrazano Narrows) to lower Manhattan [55]. It is not from the island, which is too close, nor

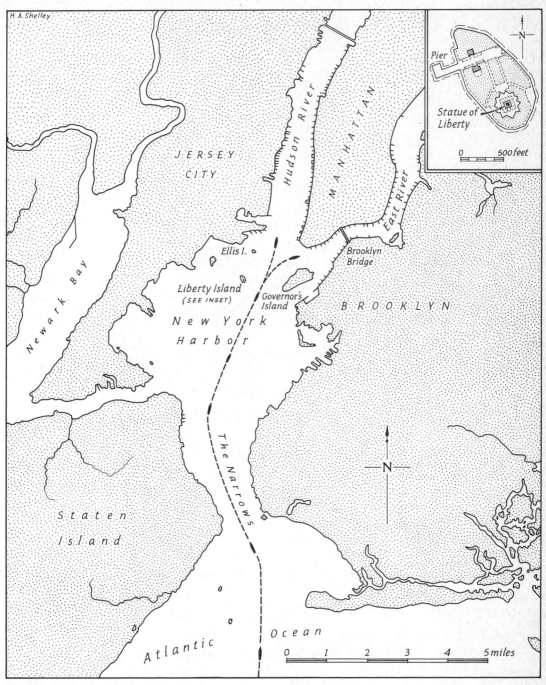

H. A. Shelley

Inset (top right):
Pier
Statue of Liberty
N
0   500 feet

Main map labels:
JERSEY CITY
Hudson River
MANHATTAN
East River
Brooklyn Bridge
Ellis I.
Liberty Island
(SEE INSET)
Governor's Island
BROOKLYN
New York Harbor
Newark Bay
The Narrows
N
Staten Island
Atlantic Ocean

0   1   2   3   4   5 miles

55. Map of New York Harbor

56 and 57. *Liberty* seen from a ship
entering New York Harbor

58 (*opposite*). *The Statue of Liberty*

from New York, which is too far away, nor from any fixed point
that one is intended to admire *Liberty*, but from a ship moving to
port across her gaze – a most unusual prospect for sculpture.
Within this trajectory there is, however, a principal if fleeting point
which is reached shortly after passing through the Narrows.
Many contemporary representations are taken exactly from this
point where *Liberty* appears to be striding powerfully forwards, the
lines and contours of her form (especially the drapery folds)
sweeping together upwards in a forceful movement to the torch
[56]. From this perspective her forward impetus is reinforced by a
strong tendency of the eye to read from left to right in a pictorial
structure (and *Liberty* in her site was conceived in broadly pictorial
terms). But as the ship passes in front of the statue a curious dualism
unfolds: the dynamic image retreats and a second figure emerges
standing still and rigidly erect [57]. As one moves on towards
Manhattan, to the end of the arc, the initial impression vanishes
altogether [58].

Bartholdi's ambition often outran his ability to conceive plastic form. This is manifest in his first important 'success', the *General Rapp* in Colmar [8]. Although clearly inspired by François Rude's convincingly heroic *Marshal Ney* (of 1853) who, it has been said, 'claims a whole army as his invisible complement', *Rapp* has an awkward spastic pose which nowhere resolves into a coherent image.[6] As the observer passes round this statue one imbalanced configuration succeeds another, yielding a flow of awkwardness very different from the magic flux of the Renaissance *figura serpentinata* which presents a cycle of harmonious views (or at least the eight viewpoints of Benvenuto Cellini's canonical compass).[7] This deformity can be observed in many of Bartholdi's more prominent statues, including the *Lafayette* in Union Square, New York [59] and, with a somewhat different mode of awkwardness, in the unintentionally mock-heroic equestrian *Vercingétorix* gracing the central square of Clermont-Ferrand, which reminded a contemporary of a horse on a merry-go-round [60].[8] The *Lion of Belfort* [10] is, however, an imposing success, for all its dependence on Thorvaldsen's *Lion of Lucerne* and despite its formal harshness. Though without anything approaching genius for sculptural form, Bartholdi was a man of considerable perception and intelligence. He realized that his place in history would depend on *Liberty* and in his apologia he quoted Charles Blanc's ominous warning to those venturing to work on a colossal scale: 'Faults once committed can be hidden by no subterfuge, and if the artist fails, the depth of his fall is commensurate with the immensity of his aspirations.'[9] He clearly wished to leave nothing to chance in shaping his most ambitious work. Not only did he model, over a period of five years, a series of maquettes for *Liberty* – only three of which are preserved – but during the process of enlarging the form and even while the full-scale work was being executed he continued to make subtle changes until practically the last rivet was in place.[10]

The development of his conception and also the origin of the formal dualism in the final work may be traced in Bartholdi's

59. *Lafayette.*
Bartholdi, 1873-6

60. *Vercingétorix.*
Bartholdi, 1869–1903

five surviving models and one drawing for the Suez project [11, 14, 15] and the three models of 1870–75 for *Liberty* herself [17–19]. The former group embodies relatively vigorous Neo-Baroque attitudes, the thrust of the torch arm countered by bodily movement and torsion, sometimes with a broad stance and the opposite arm flung back. At this stage Bartholdi seems not to have understood that strong contrapposto and projection of limbs, simple enough to execute in works of normal size, would present nightmarish structural difficulties when enlarged to colossal scale. The first *Liberty* model, though dependent on the Suez project, shows greater regard for structural feasibility in its alignment. But only in the definitive model, made when dreams threatened to become reality, did Bartholdi draw the silhouette into a closed, almost columnar form in which even the upraised arm is kept within the plan of the base. (Viollet-le-Duc, his structural adviser at the time, may well have influenced this development.) Although, by carefully arranging a helical system of lines (which look almost Gothic), swinging up diagonally through the drapery, Bartholdi achieved a dynamic impression from one viewpoint, he ironed back the Neo-Baroque sculptural conformation into the rigidly Neo-Classical columnar outline which it presents from all others. Thus it seems that the problematic dualism of image was not originally intended but emerged out of the adaptation of a preconceived form to structural contingencies.

Now, whether or not Bartholdi was conscious of this meta-morphosis during the process, he certainly must have been aware of the dualism of the final form. As an admitted admirer of 'Assyrian colossal sculpture', Bartholdi may even have realized that the already famous Assyrian type of 'five-legged' guardian creature, set like his own goddess at city gates, provided an unmistakable ancient prototype for the double image [61] that could have stimu-lated his imagination during the formative process or, at least, have helped to justify the invention in his mind *ex post facto*.[11]

61. Gateway figure from Nimrud, 883–859 B.C.

The final key to understanding *Liberty*'s formal singularity is the relationship of spectator and statue to the topography of New York harbor, a question that remains open. In this context it is crucial to observe that the kinetic image of the eye of the shipboard observer was not the only image of *Liberty*. A strong 'ideal' image of the statue in its setting existed as well, and the two images interact.

Bartholdi's view of the harbor scene – executed, to be sure, *c.* 1875, after the form of the statue had been settled [62] – depicts *Liberty* against the backdrop of New York and New Jersey, not only greatly exaggerating her scale but rotating what was already planned to be her actual position almost a quarter turn so that she stands frontally with the city directly behind her. In this vision – which obviously distorts three-dimensional realities for the sake of two-dimensional impact – *Liberty* rises as a great emblematic façade for America, in a manner that distinctly recalls the traditional

62. Project for the *Statue of Liberty*. Bartholdi, *c.* 1875

63. 'The Colossus of Rhodes' from J. B. Fischer von Erlach: *Historische Architektur*, 1721

representation of the way the most important single prototype for *Liberty* – the Colossus of Rhodes – stood before its harbor [63]. The prospect undoubtedly represented the kind of general impression Bartholdi wished his statue to make.

As much as Bartholdi probably would have preferred to erect such a frontal image, none of the sites offered the possibility. The only location that would have allowed frontality, Lower Manhattan, was out of the question: the density of buildings there would have blurred the statue's impact, and the conflict of scale would have been jarring. The colossus would have been too large for the predominantly small buildings and narrow streets, and yet too small when viewed together with the immense new bridge to Brooklyn of which Bartholdi could hardly have been unaware (the unrivaled scale of its visionary leap over the waters of the harbor may even have abetted his plan for a visionary monument rising from them). Besides, *Liberty* was meant for all America, not just New York City. Bartholdi was offered two sites by the authorities: Governor's Island and Bedloe's (now Liberty) Island.[12] He had discovered the desirability of the latter already on his visit in 1871. Although both islands have fortresses that would provide a majestic platform for the statue, not only is the Bedloe's Island fortress – Fort Wood (1808-11) – by far the more impressive, but *Liberty* rises with greater prominence from the much smaller landmass [64]. Moreover, whereas Governor's Island blurs (isthmus–like) indistinctly with New York and Brooklyn – and the Bridge – behind it, *Liberty*'s site is clearly an isolated island from every viewpoint. From the entrance to the harbor it stands against the great mouth of the Hudson River, and, moreover, lies on the direct sightline of passengers as they pass through the Narrows.

Even on Bedloe's Island *Liberty* could not stand for long in the path of the oncoming viewer on his way to the docks of New York. And if *Liberty* had been placed with her back to New York – as in the 'ideal' image – she would have faced increasingly *away* from the oncoming spectator, clearly an undesirable arrangement. In fact, the form of the star fortress on Bedloe's Island did not allow much choice in the matter, its plan not being uniformly radial. It is composed of angular bastions projecting from a roughly square core, with two bastions per side except facing the harbor channel, where one great bastion juts out. Obviously it would have been difficult – though not impossible, had it finally proved necessary – for Bartholdi *not* to have aligned his statue with the clear cross–channel directionality of the fortress.

64. Liberty Island, with New Jersey in the background

Bartholdi evidently realized that a cross-channel orientation would provide a solution to the conflict between the 'ideal' and the perceived images. The cross-channel alignment gives the spectator an initial oblique view of the statue. It has been seen how Bartholdi transformed the original dynamic *form* of the proto- and early *Liberty* maquettes into a dynamic *impression*, if viewed obliquely. The purpose (or at least the result) of this formal manipulation can now be understood: to the shipboard observer *Liberty* presents an illusion of forward movement – of striding into the path to New York (and America). Thus Bartholdi achieved – by kinetic implication if not in actuality – an ingeniously simple resolution of the 'ideal' Rhodian image with the topographic realities and the position of the spectator. He must also have appreciated the further

65. *Liberty* seen from Battery Park

virtues of this solution. For as soon as the observer pulls alongside the statue, its movement is displaced, as has been noted, by a stable – frontal – image that remains in the mind as one's attention becomes increasingly dominated by the excitement of disembarking. Finally, from Manhattan, *Liberty* looms decently – even if awkwardly – from her left, never quite turning her back on her audience [65].

Bartholdi thus chose Bedloe's Island because it was the better of the alternatives offered, and accepted the directional dictates of the fortress because he was able to find a workable formal solution, with respect both to the visual impact on the moving observer, and to the Rhodian tradition of the colossus as an emblematic façade. At the same time this site enabled Bartholdi to realize the idea that had been formulated even before he sailed to America in 1871. For even if, on the compass, *Liberty* actually faces SSE, to the spectator she *seems* to face outward towards the Atlantic and across to the Old World – the 'world' she 'enlightens' – and most specifically her proud French patrons and their audience (clearly yet another reason why Bartholdi rejected Governor's Island, where *Liberty* would have had to turn her back on Europe, as well as foregoing the natural left-to-right impetus).

Conventional aesthetic considerations apart, Bartholdi's executive competence and formal ingenuity can hardly fail to impress. His strong feeling for site and scale, image and symbol was, of course, rooted in the French tradition of planning monumental sites – one thinks of Versailles and the Place Vendôme, of the Champs Élysées, and the Place de l'Opéra. But even in Bartholdi's day of hectic monument building that sense was not so very common, and in our own time it is practically non-existent. (The landscape sculptors seem to be trying desperately to recapture it.)[13] When we descend to the most concrete of all *Liberty*'s aspects – her structure and fabrication – it is only to emerge with the strongest admiration for the skill and perseverance of Bartholdi and his colleagues.

66. Enlarging *Liberty*'s hand in plaster, 1876–81

6. Construction

The most widely appealing aspect of the *Statue of Liberty* – after the thrill of her sheer scale and the grandeur of her site – is the triumph of technique and skill involved in her construction.

The final form having been settled as of 1875 in a clay model 1.25 meters high, it was subjected to a series of three enlargements in plaster: first to 2.85 meters; then four times to about 11 meters; and finally four times again to full-scale components of the colossus, whose total height is forty-six meters from the base to the top of the torch (or thirty-four meters from the heel to the top of the head). The method of enlargement was simple in theory – taking measurements from plumb lines to points of the model, the three measurements taken for each point multiplied equally in being applied to the corresponding point on the enlarged version. If the Cartesian operation was theoretically simple, in practice it involved an immense amount of painstaking labor, for each enlargement involved more than 9,000 measurements. Moreover, each time the form was blown up visual corrections had to be made to compensate for the new effects of the old form at greatly enlarged scale – decisions that could only be entrusted to the sculptor himself [66].

Once enlarged to a full scale set of plaster fragments, there was the matter of transferring the shape to hammered copper sheets [67–8]. Carpenters constructed massive wooden forms that followed the contours of the full-scale plaster. On these forms the thin copper sheets – 2.5 mm. in thickness – were gently forced into shape by levers and hammering. As a further control, the shape of the plaster model was then pressed directly into very thin, easily malleable lead

sheets, to which the still relatively rough form of the copper was made to conform exactly.[1]

The repoussé technique chosen for *Liberty* was an ancient one. Indeed, the earliest Greek bronzes were made of hammered sheets of the metal, riveted together over a wooden core. But after casting was mastered, the hammered technique – so much clumsier and less precise – was rarely employed. However, in works of extremely large scale, where great precision was less important than cost and weight (metal can be hammered thinner than cast, which is why the gold in Phidias's chryselephantine colossi was hammered), it appears occasionally – probably in the Colossus of

Rhodes,[2] but more influentially two millennia later in the colossal *S. Carlo Borromeo*, whose form Bartholdi despised but whose hammered skin (only 1.5 mm. thick) he greatly admired.[3] Not surprisingly, the technique was revived for many nineteenth-century large-scale architectural and sculptural projects.[4] Characteristically, pure copper was used now – as it had been for the *S. Carlo Borromeo* – rather than the harder and more costly traditional alloy with tin. Perhaps the most prominent project in the medium was the never executed gargantuan Napoleonic quadriga for the Arc de Triomphe de l'Étoile. The very workshop in which *Liberty* was executed – the establishment of Gaget, Gauthier et Cie. – had produced a number of the major examples: the cupola of the new Opera (designed 1861), the statues on the spires of Notre-Dame and the Ste Chapelle (1835 ff), and the *Renommée* dominating the central pavilion of the Trocadéro Palace.[5] And there was Millet's seven-meter equestrian *Vercingétorix* of 1865, which appears to have inspired Bartholdi's project of the same subject shortly afterwards (not irrelevantly, the structural engineer of Millet's figure was Viollet-le-Duc, who advocated the employment of copper repoussé).[6] Finally, von Bandel's just completed *Arminius* confronted Bartholdi with its technique as well as its nationalist message [46].

The difference between the repoussé and cast techniques lay not only in the execution but also in their structural nature. Even a colossal sculpture could be cast with sufficient thickness – about an inch in the *Bavaria*, for example – to form a rigid shell that is essentially self-sustaining, requiring only a minimum of internal bracing, once the pieces are fastened together. Unlike such an exoskeleton, the thin skin of a large-scale hammered work has little inherent rigidity, and requires a complementary system of full internal supports. The hammered gold and thin ivory of Phidias's chryselephantine colossi rested on a substantial wooden core. Although the projecting arm of *S. Carlo Borromeo* was formed around a metal armature, his body is all but filled with a massive masonry pier [69].[7] Such relatively cumbersome solutions, relying on sheer mass for stability, were still employed in the 1870s when the builders of *Liberty* were confronted with the problem.

Liberty presented such complex difficulties that a structural specialist was called in. Her first engineer was the eminent Eugène Emmanuel Viollet-le-Duc,[8] a universal architect whose scholarly understanding of medieval architecture and theory far exceeded his abilities (and his contemporary renown and posthumous notoriety) as a practitioner and especially as a restorer. Both his interest in structural theory and his personal brand of medievalism

69. *S. Carlo Borromeo,*
diagram showing interior construction

were to play a role of some importance for *Liberty*. But he seems, initially, to have been drawn to the project for other reasons. For although under the Second Empire he was obliged to repress his political views for the most part (especially because of his close friendship with the Empress Eugénie), he remained at heart as ardent a republican as when he fought at the age of sixteen on the barricades of 1830. Later, he pushed through certain radical reforms in the structure of the Academy. In the early 1870s he re-entered the political arena, and by 1873–4 had become a staunch republican. It was this political allegiance as much as the intriguing engineering problems that drew him into the *Liberty* project of his ideological colleagues.[9]

In Viollet-le-Duc's solution to the problems of *Liberty*, his heavy-handedness in actual design and his rationalist – rather than rational – theoretical bent are confirmed. He maintained the traditional reliance on mass for stability, but instead of heavy masonry, projected 'a system of interior compartments [*cloisons*] . . . filled with sand'. His rationale: 'with masonry, if some accident occurs, demolition is necessary; whereas with the compartments, it will suffice to open a valve, set in the lower surface of each compartment, and the sand will escape by itself,' giving access, he imagined, for workmen to reach the damaged parts of the statue. This scheme, on which he was still working in 1875 when it was proudly described at the great Hôtel du Louvre banquet, which he attended, was to rise only to the hips.[10] Above, he probably planned a lighter weight construction. The *S. Carlo Borromeo* utilized an iron beam for its projecting arm, and Viollet-le-Duc's scheme for the upper body – particularly the torch arm – undoubtedly involved an open ferrous armature, perhaps resembling in technique the imaginary ironwork illustrated in his *Entretiens* (particularly in Volume II, belatedly published in 1872).[11] This armature would have formed at least temporarily the support for the two advance fragments of *Liberty* – the right hand and torch, already displayed in the 1876 Philadelphia

70. *Liberty*'s hand and torch,
Philadelphia Centennial 1876

Centennial [70], and the head, exhibited at the Paris International Fair of 1878 [71] – both chosen not only because they were the most impressive single components but also because they permitted visitors to enter and climb to a viewing platform.[12]

The Exposition Building that *Liberty*'s head temporarily ornamented in 1878 – a huge metal-and-glass construction typical of the International Fairs since London's Crystal Palace, which, like *Liberty*, was put up temporarily, taken down and moved to a permanent site – was erected by the man who was to provide her definitive structure. When Viollet-le-Duc died in 1879, the responsibility for *Liberty*'s interior passed from the hands of a

71. *Liberty's* head,
Paris Exhibition 1878

structural theoretician born in the days of Napoleon (1814) to a member of Bartholdi's generation who was among the great technicians of history, and who certainly was the most brilliant French engineer of his time. Gustave Eiffel, born in 1832, came from a long line of artisans of the *ancien régime* that had been dispersed by the Revolution and, we might note, had like Bartholdi an energetic, courageous mother, active in the economic affairs of the family, and admired by her son all his life.[13] Not only did Eiffel become a brilliant technician, but of equal importance for his astonishing line of successful projects, he was a masterful, indeed, an indomitable entrepreneur, promoter and administrator. Like Ferdinand de Lesseps (maker of Suez), who joined *Liberty*'s ranks at about the same time (after Laboulaye's death in 1883 he was head of the French *Liberty* Committee), or for that matter, R. M. Hunt, who was to do the pedestal, General Stone, who built the colossal foundations, Joseph Pulitzer, who raised the final funds, and even Bartholdi himself to some degree, Gustave Eiffel was an archetypal nineteenth-century character in his blinding self-confidence and drive. The *Statue of Liberty* was only possible in the hands of such men, the individualists that the age itself was already quite conscious of as peculiar to itself. The breed appears colorfully in various works of the contemporary writer, Jules Verne, and most melodramatically in his *Robur le Conquérant* of 1886 (tr. *The Clipper of the Clouds*).[14] Robur is the aggressive commander of a multiple helicopter with seventy-four rotors who flies around planting a black flag bearing a golden sun surrounded by stars on such spots as the highest minaret of the Hagia Sophia, the dome of St Peter's, the Eiffel Tower (in the 1891 edition), and the *Statue of Liberty* itself. Before he is destroyed by lightning, he gives a talk which embodies the essential ethos of Eiffel and his peers to an imaginary American scientific society: 'Citizens of the U.S. My name is Robur. I am worthy of that name! I am forty years old although I look but thirty, and I have a constitution of iron . . . You see before you an engineer whose nerves are in no way inferior to his muscles. I have no fear of anything or anybody . . . When I have decided on a thing, all America, all the world, may strive in vain to keep me from it.'[15]

It was inevitable that although Eiffel took his degree in chemistry at the École Centrale des Arts et Manufactures (having failed admittance to the École Polytechnique) in 1855 as preparation for entering his uncle's vinegar manufactory, he soon crossed over into greener pastures. Through a chemist's metallurgical training he was able to migrate to the ironworks, and from there to the construction of perhaps the most portentous iron structures of the time: the development of the railroad which in France was truly beginning during the Second Empire. The 'Great Iron Horse' could only pull the train up a very shallow incline – no more than 1:800 – which necessitated the cutting of hundreds of tunnels and especially the building of numerous bridges over valleys, whose size and geology taxed the abilities of the engineer to the limit. Although as early as the 1867 Paris Exposition Building Eiffel became widely involved with other aspects of civil engineering – constructing department stores, railway stations, even an observatory[16] – it was the railway bridge that embodied his essential ideas, first made his name, and provided the prototypal forms for *Liberty* (and his great tower as well).

Already in the early 1860s Eiffel was testing his ideas in a number of bridge commissions – many obtained in international competition with great European firms – accumulating as he went along a repertoire of brilliant engineering innovations: continuous girder construction of enormous length; flexible joints to allow thermal expansion and absorb the shock of the moving train; great airy, two-hinged arches erected without centering (like Brunelleschi's dome); and his specialty (most significant for *Liberty*), enormously high, spidery iron pylons. These were achieved definitively in the bridge over the Douro at Oporto in Portugal (completed 1877) and then in the even more spectacular and widely published Pont du Garabit of 1879–84 (over the Truyère at Garabit, 14 km. from St-

72. The Pont du Garabit.
Eiffel, 1879–84

Flour in the Auvergne), rising 122.5 meters above the river, almost half a kilometer in length, with the central arch spanning 165 meters [72].[17] These bridges were not only triumphs of dazzling technique and sheer scale, but of extraordinary powers of ideation in establishing the equipoise between the great continuous trellis girder of the road-bed and the pylons and arches rising up from the valley to support it, as well as the miraculous resistance of the ingeniously coordinated forms to the shock of the train and the blasts of winds sweeping through the valleys.[18]

Eiffel did not consider himself an architect, nor had he been trained as such. Unlike Viollet-le-Duc, who was still a traditional universal builder and who, we shall see, seems to have contributed the earliest architectural project for *Liberty*'s base as well as the first structural notions, Eiffel was a specialist. Even his motives for

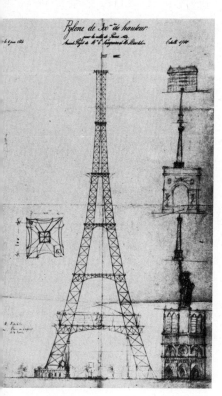

73. Project for the Tour Eiffel.
E. Nouguier and M. Koechlin, 1884

taking on the *Liberty* job were, if patriotically French, essentially apolitical, a pure engineering challenge. When his projects required 'architectural' detail, Eiffel called in an architect from his office, a specialist at decoration who could impart the traditional architectural veneer to his work. This characteristic late-nineteenth-century architectural schizophrenia – a divorce of appearance and structural reality and the processes of their design[19] – was overtly manifest in Eiffel's most famous work, the Eiffel Tower, built for the Exhibition of 1889 to 'frapper le monde' [73].[20] In structure, it is essentially a visionary extrapolation of his bridge innovations. But it was adorned with architectural metalwork frills at the first level (now unfortunately lost), and the base includes structurally superfluous forms that create the unrelated image of the largest of all triumphal arches [6]. Celebrating 'the glory of modern sciences, and for the more special honor of French industry,' it was said to form 'a triumphal arch as striking as those which earlier generations have raised to honor conquerors' (a reference to Napoleon's arch across the Seine).[21]

However different in other respects, the *Statue of Liberty* is but another example of this disjunction: Eiffel's hidden structural reality is totally unrelated to the statue's very traditional appearance. *Liberty* is an archetypal illustration of the aesthetic tension of its time – when technology had already attained great advances and power and a hold over the mind, but when the conscious eye was still dominated by traditional imagery. Although the closing decades of the century were already offered the solutions of, let us say, the Chicago and Viennese schools of architecture, only the last generation born in the century would achieve universal solutions that permeated the aesthetic structure – of most importance Cubism and the International Style, reintegrating structure and appearance by (to grossly simplify the matter) accepting the sensibility of science and the machine.[22]

That the aesthetic of the future should have been affected by the works of Eiffel – particularly his tower – is curious, because it was so unintentional. Eiffel's conscious taste was very conventional not only in the 'architecture' with which he clothed his pristine engineering, but in the pompous furnishings he surrounded himself with (even in his 'laboratory' atop the tower).[23] Yet his constructions, especially those bereft of the dubious benefits of an 'architect's' collaboration, invariably are of an extraordinary daring, elegance and refinement in their calculus, geometry and detail. The resultant purity and harmony of forms of visionary scale, such as in the Garabit Bridge or the piers of the tower, approach true sublimity.[24]

There is a style to Eiffel's works that is more than just a reflection of the universal methods of the engineering discipline. If not entirely personal, it seems at least inherently French. This is immediately apparent in even a brief comparison of his oeuvre with the heavy-handedness of contemporary German bridges, such as the Emperor William Bridge over the Wimper of 1897,[25] a travesty of the Garabit Bridge, or with the brutalist British forms such as the monstrous (and glorious) Firth of Forth Bridge (1883-9).[26] The most famous of all modern bridges, *Liberty*'s nearly exact contemporary, the Roeblings' Brooklyn Bridge of 1869-83, with its unprecedented span of 1600 feet, relies for stability not so much on ingenuity of form or geometry, but on a thick accumulation of elements – the great catenary curve, the cross cables, the sheer mass of the roadbed[27] – so fundamentally different in ideation and appearance from the seemingly weightless equipoise of Eiffel's works (which is not to deny the bridge's own celebrated beauty). Through the sheer magic of geometry Eiffel could build even more airily than the Gothic architects of his native Burgundy and yet with tremendous strength.[28]

Even for Eiffel the problem of *Liberty*'s armature was not an easy one. Its every component, down to the smallest rivet, was precisely calculated with the techniques of mathematic analysis and graphic statics developed in the previous half century[29] that he had long mastered [74-6]. But this did not mean that the solution was a foregone conclusion. With the exception of the primary structure – a pylon directly adapted from his bridges – almost everything else called for new design. The giant statue was, after all, a rather different configuration from a railway bridge (or any of the other types of architectural construction Eiffel was familiar with). Her fragile skin needed support not only against gravity but against the high winds of New York harbor that would buffet the great surface, far larger than any sail. Although Bartholdi had finally compressed the figure into a broadly columnar form, her local foldwork was extremely complicated and there was, moreover, the torch arm that still swung out from the line of the body at a precarious angle.

74. Calculations for *Liberty*'s armature. Eiffel, *c.* 1880

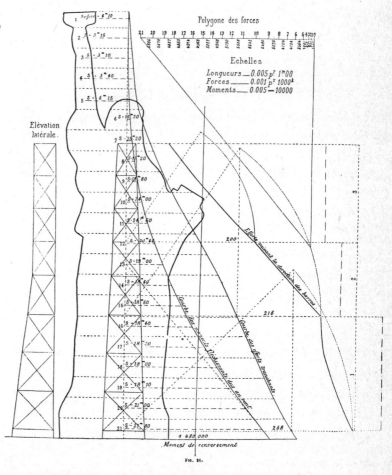

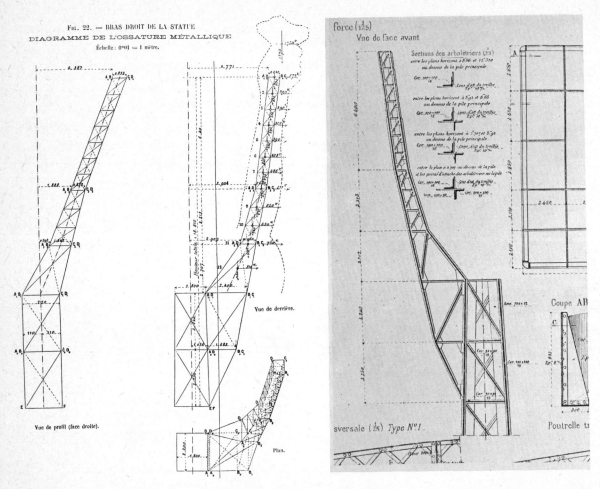

75 (*left*). Calculations for the armature of *Liberty*'s arm. Eiffel, *c.* 1880

76 (*above*). Design for the armature of *Liberty*'s arm. Eiffel, *c.* 1880

Eiffel's structural core is a wrought-iron pylon 29.54 meters high, tapering from a base plan of 5.3 by 4.2 meters to 2.2 by 1.8 meters at the top. The corner piers are massive angle girders, 70 by 60 centimeters in section, assembled of iron plates 12–15 millimeters in thickness and including, at the outer corners, supplementary projecting angle beams for the attachment of the bracing and secondary structure. Such angles, fabricated in pairs to form T-shaped beams, serve for the nine levels of horizontal struts and also for the crucial double diagonal bracing that laces the entire pylon into a powerful, rigid trussed unit [77]. On its

77. *Liberty*'s armature in construction. Paris 1881–4

upper two levels is hung the more complex trussed asymmetrical girder that swings out and rises a total of 19.81 meters (12.38 meters above the top of the pylon) to form the core of the torch arm. Here angles are combined in pairs and fours (to form cross-shaped beams) for the cross-braced rising members, in this case complemented by massive platework reinforcement that yields a dense, extremely powerful beam that narrows as it reaches up to the torch [78, 79]. The extraordinary resiliency of the pylon and arm structure can be strongly felt by anyone foolish enough to

78A and B.
Liberty in course of construction. Paris 1881–4

79. *Liberty* delivered to the American Ambassador in Paris, 4 July 1884

80. View from *Liberty*'s torch

stand on the torch on a gusty day, where one senses the 43 meter armature responding like a giant, powerfully elastic spring to the buffeting of the wind [80].[30]

Although less obvious in its boldness, the connection of the pylon to the skin of the statue was at least equally inventive. From the massive central tower a secondary system of lightweight trusswork – single angles throughout – reaches out on all sides towards the interior surface of the figure [77, 81]. Points of attachment are provided on the copper skin itself by an inner webbing of strapwork (18 by 50 millimeters in thickness) which acts to consolidate the thin membrane as well. This secondary trusswork is joined to the

81. *Liberty*'s interior, showing the linkage between trusswork and the statue

82. *Liberty*'s interior, showing secondary trusswork and linkage to strapwork (view down)

webbed skin not by rigid connections, but by what amounts to a tertiary level of structure: thin, flat iron bars, attached at their lower end by a single bolt to the secondary trusswork and at their upper end to a convenient point of the strapwork [81, 82]. It is these simple connections which are, in fact, the most ingenious and subtle aspect of the entire armature. Bending upwards and outwards towards the skin, the thin bars are nothing but simple springs. The skin, in other words, is not rigidly attached to the armature, but floats at the ends of hundreds of flexible members that form a suspension to which the entire skin adheres. Floating thus on springs, the thin copper envelope is given an extraordinarily supple elasticity, allowing it to adjust subtly to thermal expansion and contraction and yet resist the pressures of the winds acting unevenly on the sculpted surfaces (probably the major reason why most of *Liberty*'s carefully countersunk rivets are still intact).[31]

All iron construction involves problems of thermal expansion; and the larger the structure, the greater the difficulties. Thus flexible joints of various kinds were pioneered, for example, by such prominent engineers as De Dion and Contamin in the 1870s and 1880s for their enormous exhibition halls.[32] We have noted that hinged joints were of particular importance to Eiffel in his railway bridges, where, in addition to thermal and atmospheric stresses, there was the shock of the massive, rapidly moving train. What was particularly ingenious about *Liberty*'s solution was the cunning realization that the simplest possible member – an elemental bar that could itself bend one way and pivot in the other direction around its single point anchorage to the trusswork – not only yielded a flexible and economic means of attachment, but could be relied upon to achieve the necessary rigidity of form when acting in the hundreds in conjunction with the sheer tensile cohesion of the suspended, webbed skin. With an uncanny prophecy of stressed-skin construction that would become crucial in twentieth-century aeronautic engineering (in airplane wings, for example), Eiffel realized that as a totality the secondary and tertiary elements of his wrought-iron armature together with Bartholdi's thin copper envelope – forms relatively fragile in isolation – would generate a structural cohesion far greater than the sum of the individual strengths of its parts. Once again Eiffel conceived the very kind of visionary equipoise that had enabled his bridges, and later his tower, to stand.

The intrinsic genius of the solution appears to have escaped all who commented on the structure, which was widely published at the time and explained merely as a simple extrapolation of Eiffel's railway piers. However, in one respect American builders, at least, may have learned a lesson. All could see that no part of *Liberty*'s shell rests directly on the parts below, being instead hung entirely on the iron skeleton. *Liberty* was thus, even if in the form of a statue, among the first great curtain wall constructions. In this, as well as in the detail of Eiffel's trusswork, American builders could have found inspiration, for *Liberty* was put up in the very years that the problems of the skyscraper were being confronted in Chicago, Cincinnati, and New York (a field in which the designer of the pedestal, R. M. Hunt, was active).[33]

The structure of the base also presented difficult technical problems. As we have already seen, the responsibility of the French was limited to the statue itself. Everything below – site, foundations, and pedestal – was in the hands of the Americans. In 1877 the great Civil War figure, General Sherman, was finally appointed to decide whether Bedloe's or Governor's Island – both federal property – would be the location of the colossus. For reasons already noted, Bartholdi had fallen in love with the former alternative on his 1871 trip (although not immediately upon entering the harbor, as he later boasted), and now Sherman hospitably deferred to the sculptor's wishes.[34]

Foundation work for the project began in 1883, concurrently with the erection of the statue itself in Paris (1881–4). In charge of construction was General Charles P. Stone, another Civil War veteran, well known for his exploits in the Sudan for Ismail Pasha during the very years when Bartholdi was seeking work from him. At the center of the fortress a huge, square pit was excavated, with considerable difficulty because of massive earlier agglomerate substructures, which, however, ultimately added to the final stability. The foundation itself is an enormous tapering block of concrete, 53 feet deep, 91 feet square at the bottom, and 65 feet square at the top (and with only a ten-foot-square open shaft in the center). The pedestal above is constructed of massive walls (from eight to nineteen feet in thickness) that continue the battered line of the truncated pyramidal substructures, tapering from 65 feet square at the bottom to 43 feet at the foot of the statue (with a central opening 27 feet square) [83]. Like the foundation, the pedestal walls are of concrete, with only the external architectural detail in granite masonry (quarried from Leete's Island, Connecticut). As was the case with skeletal iron construction, *Liberty's* modern concrete technology was first pioneered in Europe and used, for example, extensively by Haussmann in his rebuilding of Paris. Although it was employed on an increasing scale in the United States after the mid-century, *Liberty's* foundations and pedestal constituted by far the largest single concrete mass of its time (more than 27,000 tons). In fact, by its very magnitude and its international prominence, the large-scale employment of concrete at the statue appears to have marked a turning point in the United States in the revival of the ancient Roman building material.[35]

However massive and monolithic, concrete was technically artificial stone, and, like all stone, had a high compressive strength but a relatively low tensile resistance. It is this factor which has always limited spans in trabeated masonry, such as the inter-columnar distance in the Greek orders. Traditionally, this weakness had been marginally compensated by the not uncommon employment of reinforcing metal components. In the closing decades of the nineteenth century this traditional combination found its modern form in reinforced concrete, or artificial stone with steel members bonded in its core.[36] At the *Statue of Liberty* a kind of

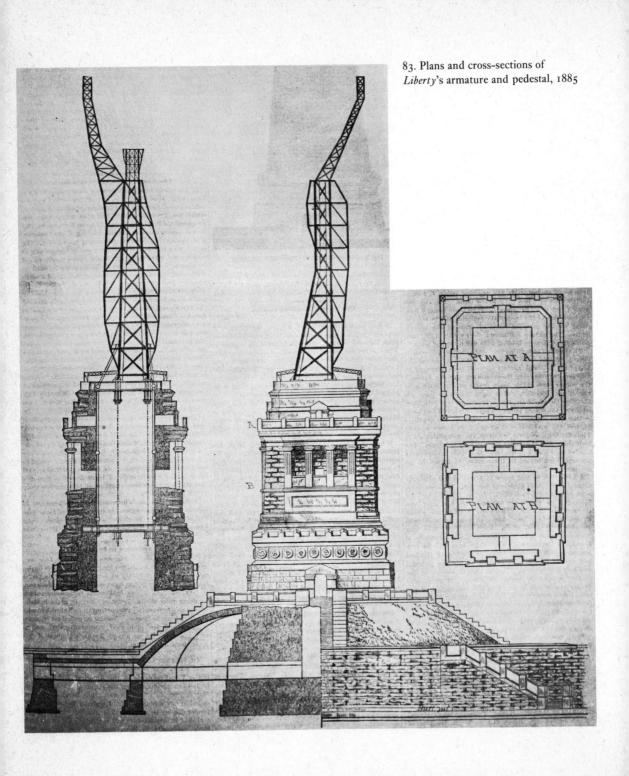

83. Plans and cross-sections of *Liberty*'s armature and pedestal, 1885

transitional method was employed. At the foot of the pedestal a horizontal cross-yoke of massive pairs of triple steel I-beams are laid wall to wall, with a matching set similarly embedded in the masonry at the top. These are connected by proportionately powerful steel girders running up along the interior of all four walls [83].[37] This has two essential results. The massive compressive strength of the concrete-and-masonry pedestal is reinforced by powerful tensile members. And the upper cross-yoke provides unyielding points of attachment for Eiffel's armature (by means of massive bolts). The total structure is so firm that it was said – with only a degree of hyperbole – that to overturn the statue one would have to upturn the island itself.

The combined work of Stone, Eiffel and Bartholdi forms an impressive structural sequence, indeed, an integrated, hierarchical organism (not unlike some giant plant or flower). A massive concrete block is set into the earth, carrying a great hollow trunk above, which is consolidated and locked firmly to the powerful wrought-iron pylon of Eiffel by brawny steel members. Secondary trusswork reaches out from this elegant tower towards the inner surface of the sculpture, with a tertiary structural level of springs effecting an elastic connection with the vein-like interior webbing of wrought-iron strapwork. The skin itself is a fragile, delicately suspended copper membrane only 2.5 millimeters in thickness. The unity is that of the universal methods of the civil engineer, Eiffel solving the structural needs of Bartholdi's sculptural envelope, and Stone providing the support for Eiffel's armature.

Thus far we have been concerned with the interior of the statue from a purely structural point of view and only the exterior from a visual one. But the interior was, from the first, intended to be experienced first hand by the visitor to the statue, by means of a double helical stair at the center of the pylon, one stair for those ascending to the head, the other for those returning. The climb involves a strong sensation of disorientation, for the form of the statue that seems so simple from the outside is baffling from the

interior. As one winds up the 168 stairs one has the impression
of being entangled in some gigantic structural machinery, as if
lost, perhaps, in a Jules Verne novel – halfway between Piranesi's
Prisons and the factory scene in Charlie Chaplin's *Modern Times*.

In the head of the statue, the visitor is confronted with a most
unsettling architectural apparition: a freely expressive iron structural skeleton (the spider-like cage running just within the contour
of the cranium), and the formal dominance of highly fluid and
extensive curvilinear patterns, cut by a band of fenestration that
sweeps across one half the room [84, 85]. These are none other than
the constituents of the classical Art Nouveau of such masters as
Guimard and Horta. However, the first authentic Art Nouveau

84. Interior of *Liberty*'s head

structure is Horta's house in the Rue de Turin in Brussels of 1892–3. Even lesser Art Nouveau objects go back only to the early 1880s.[38] *Liberty*'s head was not only designed in the mid 1870s but exhibited prominently at the 1878 Paris Fair - so that the extant structure of the head is probably Viollet-le-Duc's, retained in the final version for reasons of economy.[39] What is one to make of this precocious Art Nouveau apparition?

Simple analysis tells us that it involves an accidental conjunction of two forms, the iron skeleton and the inner surface of the copper envelope, that were never intended to be visually connected, and, moreover, which were each in themselves forms of completely unintentional appearance. The skeleton was determined by mathe-

85. Interior of *Liberty*'s head, looking towards the rear

matical calculations, visual considerations being of little account. The copper skin was worked into the regular patterns of the antique coiffure of the goddess, which at a normal viewing distance forms about as hair-like a feature as such a monstrous lady could possess. Seen up close and from the negative side, the hair creates a powerfully felt enclosure that seems worked into the rhythms of the sea.

This uncanny conjunction – which might be called Accidental Art Nouveau – was not without a certain timeliness. Viollet-le-Duc's theoretical projects and Eiffel's great formulations in iron and steel are in the mainstream of the current of open-linear structure leading to Art Nouveau (as is indeed Bartholdi's own balustrade of *Liberty*'s torch a proto-Art Nouveau form).[40] If the statue's classical coiffure would seem dissociated from its fortuitous internal effect, let us not forget that, as one critic emphasized, 'it is the woman who dominates the Art Nouveau world and the aspect of woman which preoccupies the artist is her hair – long, flowing hair which may . . . become part of a general wavy configuration.'[41]

Most visitors to the head of *Liberty*, however, neglect its appearance in their eagerness to see the view of the harbor from the diadem windows, the sensation intensified by the consciousness that – like the Lilliputians atop Gulliver's head – one is looking out from the vantage point of a giant (thus for a glorious moment *becoming* the colossus). For in addition to its abstract symbolism, *Liberty* exercises a powerful attraction on the child that remains in us all, like some giant toy or trick box, the expectation of which still contributes much to the gleam in the eyes of those who daily crowd aboard the ferries to Liberty Island.[42]

Almost all the large nineteenth-century monuments provided such viewing platforms – the Nelson and Bastille Columns, the *Virgin* of Le Puy (somewhat awkwardly), the *Bavaria*; even at the Arc de Triomphe de l'Étoile where the view from the top substitutes for the giant quadriga intended for the spot. Not without connection was the phenomenal popularity of ballooning in the last third of the century, for sheer amusement as well as for military and scientific purposes. The rage of the 1878 Paris Fair was the huge captive balloon controlled by a cable worked by a steam engine. Such captive balloons, however, presented the obvious dangers of collapse or gas explosion. It was therefore not to be unexpected that a fixed viewing platform of truly visionary height would appear. So it was that the greatest fulfillment of the nineteenth century love of immoderate amusements was to be the Eiffel Tower.[43]

The history of the *Statue of Liberty* cannot be properly understood without some account of Eiffel's other spectacular Parisian construction of the 1880s. Its prehistory is worth recounting. The idea of erecting a 1000 foot tower was not a new one. Already latent in certain late eighteenth-century schemes of Boullée, it emerged in the project of 1833 of the Englishman Richard Trevithick (designer of the first steam locomotive) for a cast-iron cone, 100 feet in diameter at the base and 1000 feet high, in honor of the Reform Act of the previous year. It was to be topped by a huge capital with a viewing platform 50 feet in diameter, carrying an allegorical statue 40 feet high. The notion was revived a generation later by a pair of American engineers, Clarke and Reeves, who proposed a huge iron cylinder, again 1000 feet high (revealing an almost medieval fascination with numbers), to include four galleries and many elevators, this time for the Philadelphia Centennial of 1876 for which *Liberty* had originally been intended (and where the torch was actually shown). In 1881 – when the first rivet of *Liberty*'s trial erection in Paris was being set – the idea finally migrated to France. The architects Bourdais and Sébillot proposed a masonry 'Column of the Sun', with a powerful light that would pass through a system of parabolic mirrors for the illumination (this time literal) of Paris.[44]

Four years later, his famous Garabit Bridge complete, the *Statue of Liberty* on the way to America, Eiffel took up the scheme, proposing now a metal construction to celebrate the 1889 French Centennial. He met enthusiastic response from the French state (which at the last minute had officially joined *Liberty*'s patronage), still in the flush of republican victory, and, with the French economy and industry now in ascendancy, fully appreciative of Eiffel's stated object: 'To show to the whole world that France is still a great country, and that she is still capable of success where others have failed.'[45] A competition was held and some 700 projects were submitted, of which eighteen were considered. The victorious Eiffel raced the tower to completion in less than two years after signing the contract in 1887.[46]. Although Eiffel and his apologists stressed its scientific possibilities as an observatory, and so forth (like the justifications of the moon landings, as if the public really cared about the few small rocks brought back and the contraptions left behind there) it was clearly the sheer celebrative scale and the vertiginous vista that captured everyone's imagination. One meets continuous pronouncements of the fact that the tower – which, one is assured, could easily be extended from its 984 feet to the magic English number – was twice as tall as almost any previous structure (a notable exception being the Washington Monument of 555 feet begun in 1848 but just completed in December 1884). One of the early drawings from Eiffel's office includes alongside the projected tower, to give a sense of scale, the famous structures of Paris surmounting each other – including Notre-Dame, the Arc de Triomphe, the Vendôme and July Columns, and the *Statue of Liberty* [73].

Eiffel, like Bartholdi, by the 1880s at least, was in love not only with modern science and technology, but with the colossal. In a newspaper interview in much the same vein as Bartholdi's tract, he states: 'There is in the colossal an attraction, a particular charm, to which the theories of ordinary art are hardly applicable. Does one suppose that it is by their *aesthetic* value that the Pyramids have struck man's imagination so strongly? . . . Who is the visitor who remains cold in their presence? Who has not returned from them filled with an irresistible admiration?'[47] His intoxication led him on to an outburst defending himself from the (justifiably violent) protest of the cultural establishment against the Tower's abuse of the old scale of the city.[48] Appealing to 'the people' he continued, 'The Tower will be the highest edifice ever constructed by man . . . And why should what is admirable in Egypt become hideous and ridiculous in Paris? I have searched and I avow that I don't know . . .' A typical engineer, Eiffel manifests a total insensitivity – like the modern highway builder – to the effect of his construction on the traditional fabric of human life. He is fully enraptured by the tower as the sheer material triumph of France, technology, and himself. But a true man of his era, Eiffel's visionary ecstasy achieves its culmination in his evocation – charged with the technological aesthetic and the nineteenth-century sensibility for the spectacular, indeed, the confusion of the spectacular with the beautiful – of the experience of the essential participants in his work: 'The visitors who go to the top of the tower have beneath their eyes a magnificent panorama. At their feet they see the great city, with its innumerable monuments, its avenues, its towers, and its domes, the Seine, which winds through it like a long ribbon of steel [!] . . . Paris with all its lights is like a fairyland, but in this aspect it has hitherto been known only to aeronauts, on whom its beauty has always made a strong impression. The construction of the Tower will enable thousands to contemplate a spectacle of new and incomparable loveliness.'[49]

Great entrepreneur that he was, Eiffel had his finger on the pulse of the true sensibility of his times. The tower, put up in defiance of the cultural establishment, was an inordinate success, so much so that, unlike all the other constructions of the great Paris exhibitions of the century (except the technically conservative Grand Palais), some of which were of immense structural ambition, it alone has remained standing, dominating Paris as the *Statue of Liberty* was imagined, at least, visually to control the entrance to the New World. Interestingly, the tower was going up just at the moment when *Liberty*, which had awed Paris for two years, was taken down for shipment. Indeed, it would not be unfair to say that the tower was the true French sequel to Bartholdi's statue.[50] Both belonged to the great visionary tradition. The colossus, for reasons we have observed, was exported; but the great abstraction was allowed to remain on French soil and be taken into the soul of France.

7. The Pedestal

86. Project for the *Statue of Liberty*.
Bartholdi, *c.* 1875.
Pedestal probably after Viollet-le-Duc.

If the support of the statue represents the new technology of iron and concrete, then the formal shaping of the pedestal manifests many of the rich cross-currents of contemporary architecture. The executed pedestal was the last of a line of projects by several of the principals in *Liberty*'s genesis. And it was not by any means the most distinguished of them, though it did, perhaps, embody the prevailing taste most clearly.

The earliest preserved plan appears in the publication of the *Liberty* project in 1875: a battered, massively rusticated hexagonal tower, crowned by strongly projecting, pointed corbel arches [86].[1] The form rises like a medieval keep above the fortress, and there is every reason to suppose that *Liberty*'s first structural engineer, Viollet-le-Duc, the master medieval archaeologist who in those very years was still continuing his restorations of Carcassone and the Château of Pierrefonds, had a hand in the design.

The drawing is rather rough and awkward. Indeed, it looks almost like a tentative idea. However, it was an established project, appearing on the Philadelphia Centennial Medal of 1876.[2] While its uneasy stylistic relationship to the statue might be attributed to Viollet-le-Duc's ineptitude as a designer, the problem that he faced in fashioning a pedestal was not the relatively simple matter that one might suppose.

Functionally, a pedestal is analogous to a picture frame: it isolates a work both physically and symbolically. In the typical classicizing monument of the nineteenth century, as well as in academic texts (such as Quatremère de Quincy's *Dictionnaire* entry),[3] it derives from that relationship between the pedestal and column proper in the Ionic and Corinthian orders. In such monuments the pedestal is retained in its general – or even specific – outline, and the sculpture substitutes for the column, the general proportional relationship being preserved. In painting, the frame can sometimes be far more than a mere means of achieving aesthetic detachment – as in the Sistine Ceiling. It may itself develop as a valid statement, coordinated in meaningful ways with the central painted image. Similarly, a pedestal may achieve an importance equal to, or even surpassing the sculpture it supports. Perhaps the archetypal instance of this tendency (manifest in every age, particularly late periods) is the Mausoleum of Halicarnassus, which finds a singularly impressive (and little known) post-antique counterpart in Guernieri's fantastic early-eighteenth-century *Hercules* at Wilhelmshöhe above Kassel [43].[4]

Naturally in monuments of ordinary size – as in most of Bartholdi's works – the normal pedestal is prevalent. However, the larger the statue, the greater the temptation to treat the pedestal not as a subordinate set of classicizing forms, but more ambitiously as symbolic architecture in its own right. This occurs in several of the nineteenth-century examples of colossal statuary we have discussed. Schwanthaler's *Bavaria* transformed the earlier U-shaped stoa of von Klenze into a brilliant Neo-Classical frame for herself, while Friedrich Wilhelm IV's colossus was to be set over an enormous, peripteral structure, undoubtedly with provision for the idolization of the great ruler depicted, and embodying his presence as the temples of the ancients embodied the gods whose cult images they contained. *Arminius* rises over a huge architectural curiosity (related to the Tomb of Theodoric in Ravenna) that was intended to suggest the architecture of his barbarian culture.[5]

The awkward tension of Viollet-le-Duc's project for *Liberty*'s substructure resulted from his attempt to combine both alternatives, establishing the image of an independent architectural form – a fortified tower – but distorting it into the battered, trabeated lines of the academic pedestal. The same tension characterizes the executed pedestal of Richard Hunt, who if less influential than Viollet-le-Duc, was certainly more adept at the drafting board. However, the problem was not due to any inadequacy of the designers: it was inherent in *Liberty*'s scale and site.

The *Liberty* project presented a uniquely ambiguous situation. The fortress from which the statue was to rise is manifestly of a monumental scale (though to what degree is not clear from a distance, due to the lack of detail). The colossal statue, on the other hand, is without inherent scale at all. Yet it required a pedestal of appropriately colossal dimensions. Simply to enlarge a standard Neo-Classical pedestal – as was done for the *Bavaria* – although maintaining the subordinate relationship to the sculpture, would fail to establish adequate scale for the statue and would also be incongruous with the fort. For no matter how large its actual dimensions, the traditional pedestal has sub-architectural scale, while the Bedloe Island fortress is irreducibly monumental architecture, and heavily rusticated at that. The pedestal was caught between the conflicting demands of the fortress and the colossus: it had to be grandly architectural, and yet maintain the character of a pedestal and especially its subordinate relationship to the statue, which it must not eclipse by its own grandeur. Clearly this was a very thin line for the architect to tread. On the one side was the pit of sheer formal infelicity, and on the other the sirens of ambition beckoned the designer to offer a project not only of architectural pretension, but of a powerful symbolism that would rival Bartholdi's.

Viollet-le-Duc seems to have been drawn both ways simultaneously. Perhaps he hoped to redeem the formal awkwardness of his tower by its transformation of the whole complex into what can only be described as a 'Fortress of Liberty'.[6] Although his notion

87. Pedestal project
for *Liberty*.
Bartholdi, *c*. 1880

was rejected after his death in 1879, his successors were soon to return to him for inspiration.

An alternative to Viollet-le-Duc's concept is preserved in a Bartholdi drawing in Colmar [87]. Instead of attempting to fuse contrary forms, he cleverly avoids the dilemma by separating the substructure into two components (as did von Bandel in a more awkward way): a huge stepped pyramid, rising from behind a richly decorated precinct wall; and on its truncated top, a low, well-mannered classical pedestal rising to the level of the theoretical apex of the pyramid. The massing is large enough to raise the statue to a sufficient viewing height and to give it a proper counter-balance; yet because of its interrupted silhouette the base remains subordinate. Although broad and massive, the compound design lifts dynamically, the inclined steps rippling up from behind the parapet, and the compact plasticity of the pedestal proper yielding an additional upward thrust from behind the second parapet, in a rhythmic rising movement towards the statue. The prominence of details of inherent scale – doorways, steps, parapets – lends an unequivocal colossal scale to the whole. As an architect the sculptor seems for once to have surpassed himself.

Bartholdi's sources were to some extent within his familiar ranges. For the pedestal, with its prominent Doric frieze, he had the two monuments at either end of the great urban axis on the right bank in Paris – the attic of the Arc de Triomphe de l'Étoile, and the pedestal of the July Column. The stepped pyramid brings to mind two famous ancient monuments: the upper zone of the Mausoleum of Halicarnassus (whose reconstruction was a battle-ground for archaeologists at the time) where a low pedestal for the great quadriga was set over a truncated pyramid; and the first great monument of all, Zoser's tomb at Saqqara. Yet Bartholdi may also have had a more fitting reference in mind. The reverse of the great seal of the United States (which can be seen on any dollar note) shows a stepped pyramid, its thirteen stages repre-senting the original colonies whose act of independence is alluded to by the inscription MDCCLXXVI at the foot and whose open-ended future was marked by the truncated top, above which hovers, within the theoretical line of completion of the triangle, the 'Eye of Providence' emanating an aureole of light. The structure is sited, moreover, in what appears to be a sea-like desert.[6A]

The late-eighteenth-century ideal of an architecture whose image explicitly symbolizes its program – an *architecture parlante* – had not been lost on *Liberty*'s makers, men steeped in current academic ideology, which had assimilated the revolutionary impulse. The aura of Boullée hangs about nearly all the pedestal projects, in the awkward medievalism of Viollet-le-Duc's 'Fortress of Liberty', and with far greater richness in Bartholdi's notion, which seems to embody his decades of aspirations towards the ancient world, his longings for the colossal, and his romance with America. But improbable as it might seem, Bartholdi's pyramidal concept was to be equalled, if not surpassed, in symbolic ingenuity by the master American architect who within a few years after Viollet-le-Duc's death was given charge of the pedestal – thus completing the movement towards fragmentation of planning in the hands of various specialists.

Richard M. Hunt was the first American to matriculate at the École des Beaux Arts; under his Parisian master, the prominent Lefuel, he was given charge of the construction of the Pavillon de la Bibliothèque of the New Louvre already in the early 1850s (its only error, he boastfully admitted years later, was that 'The Ionic Order on the second storey is a little slim').[7] After the Civil War Hunt was commissioned by many great New York families to build their opulent city palaces and Newport 'cottages', and he pursued in addition numerous large commercial and cultural projects, which he executed with an awesome eclectic facility. Awarded innumerable honors (including the first gold medal ever conferred upon an American by the R.I.B.A.), and a great force in the growth of the American Institute of Architects, Hunt was by

the end of the 1870s the acknowledged dean of American architecture (Baron Heinrich von Geymüller was to call him 'the
Brunellesco of the United States'[8]). He was, indeed, uniquely well
trained in the history, theory, and practice of architecture, and
his energy and industry were complemented by a remarkable
social agility and easy manner of compliance with the building
ambitions of his patrons, which is not to say that he was without
talent or imagination. Culturally, of course, Hunt was an ardent
Francophile – and, interestingly, an admirer of Viollet-le-Duc,
whom he visited on several occasions (including a stay at Pierrefonds
in 1874). So it was natural that the New York establishment would
see to it that the *Liberty* project ended in his hands.[9]

The appointment was fitting in a way that Hunt's admirers
could hardly have been fully conscious of, for he was what one can
only call an American architectural counterpart of Bartholdi
(although comparatively more prominent). Not only his career,
but even much of his personal history was analogous. Hunt came
of solid, old New England stock. Like Bartholdi, he lost his father
at an early age. He also had a temperamentally problematic and
more inherently artistic elder brother. Both Bartholdi and Hunt
found their way to fame not through artistic genius, but by providing society with pompous monuments to itself – Bartholdi, to
the proud bourgeois towns of Second Empire and Third Republic
France; Hunt, to the inordinately rich New York capitalists of the
postwar era. They were both committed to academic procedure
and the satisfactions of their patrons rather than to the fulfillment
of any abiding personal artistic vision. But perhaps their deepest
affinities lay in the extent of their ambition and the degree to which
it outdistanced artistic talent.

By 1881, Bartholdi – who would have encountered Hunt in
New York (if not in Paris), especially during his well publicized
1876 visit – was in contact with him about the specifics of the
project.[10] In 1882, in response to a letter in which Bartholdi

appears to have included sketches of his most recent ideas for the
pedestal [88, 89], Hunt's first designs took shape.[11] Although there
was still some consideration of a pyramidal project – with the
notion of a shift to a more 'appropriate' Pre-Columbian type [89][12] –
by and large Hunt seemed predisposed to return to the tower-like,
high narrow massing that had been the first official project.
Bartholdi's pyramid, after all, looked fine on paper in the Paris
atelier. But Hunt, working in sight of Bedloe's Island, soon realized

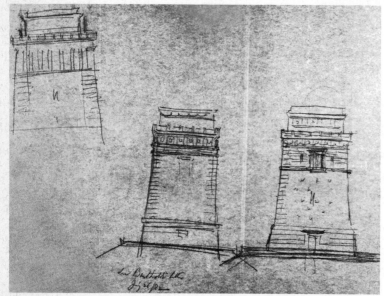

88 and 89. Pedestal projects
for *Liberty*.
Probably by Bartholdi, 1882

it would look squat on its site above Fort Wood whose powerful star-shaped thrusting outwards of great bastions invited a counter-poised clear upward thrust. The massive rustication of the fortress, moreover, would conflict with Bartholdi's smooth surfaces and fussy Neo-Classical detail. On the other hand, although Hunt felt that Viollet-le-Duc's instinct had thus been right – that a high narrow massing of strong texture was necessary – he avoided any suggestion of neo-medievalism, for if 'the Brunellesco of the United

90 and 91. Pedestal projects for *Liberty*. R. M. Hunt, 1882–3

States' developed one stylistic commitment, it was increasingly against the medieval revival and in favor of any form of classicism, even if it be the French Renaissance (François I) style that he brought enthusiastically to New York with all its hidden but strong Late Gothic aspects. Thus the considerable variety of tower-like alternatives that appear among Hunt's early drawings for the project – ranging from a classically rusticated cylinder [90] to a three-storied, richly articulated square form over a colonnaded, temple-like base [91] – all scrupulously avoid overt medievalism, while at the same time conscientiously achieving a strong texture with an eye to the fortress.

By 1883 a new project emerged in drawings and a detailed model
[92, 93]. A broad platform with battered walls (the remnant of
Bartholdi's pyramid?) lifts the pedestal into view from behind the
walls of the fortress, with straight stairs up the center of each side.
The pedestal itself, square in plan, presents a subtly tapering form
about twice as high as it is wide at the base. The great mass – 114 feet
high – assumes powerful definition and texture. For its socle Hunt
appropriates the low Doric pedestal topping out Bartholdi's
pyramid (and appearing also in some of Hunt's preparatory
drawings), giving it on each side the sub-Doric portal of Bartholdi's

92. Project 'Pharos I'.
R. M. Hunt, 1883

93. 'Pharos I' model.
R. M. Hunt, 1883

main entrances (a form going back to Boullée and Ledoux, who used it memorably in prison projects).[13] The main body of the pedestal is distinguished by two features: a triple balcony or loggia set towards the top of each side; and an intricate rustication from which blocks project in a checkerboard pattern. The structure ends with a densely sculptural terminal cornice, carrying pointed battlements, that repeats the cornice of the socle below.

What could be regarded as the failure of the earlier projects had incited Hunt to an intense effort to solve the problems that had beset his predecessors, and, with one flaw, he succeeded. Rejecting Bartholdi's composite pyramidal massing, Hunt found himself transforming Viollet-le-Duc's inept medieval conformation into a rigorously disciplined, yet powerfully expressive form that is uninhibitedly monumental architecture – its grand scale strongly rendered by the portals and the loggias – and yet at the same time recognizably but unobtrusively a pedestal, with that form's traditional socle, battered shaft, and cornice all present but tightly controlled. Of the three pedestal designers Hunt was the only actual product of the École (Bartholdi and Viollet-le-Duc having been trained in private ateliers), and it is here apparent just how well an architect could be served by the refined planning methods and formal standards of the French classical tradition.

It seems, however, that Hunt had more in mind than the mere refinement of abstract design. As with his predecessors, the symbolic potential of the grandiose project seems to have proved irresistible. In Hunt's case, the architectural symbolism centers on the manipulation of a prominent detail. The regular, alternating rows of strongly projecting blocks that dominate the surface present an unfamiliar variation in the tradition of rusticated masonry. Hunt was far too scholarly for the pattern – which immediately strikes one as a quotation – to be sheer invention.[14] Most probably it represents a combination of sources.

In the Italian and French traditions there appears a rusticated bonded masonry (stonework alternating stretchers, or long blocks laid parallel to the surface, and headers, laid into the wall with the square ends showing). Serlio, the great exponent of rustication, instrumental in its appearance in the France of François I (whose architecture was prominently revived by Hunt at just this time), advocated faceted ('diamond-cut') bonded rustication as the most advanced type. The form invited decorative variation, such as the species appearing in fortification, where the square headers take hemispherical bosses in imitation of cannonballs, as seen at Antonio da Sangallo the Younger's Fortezza da Basso in Florence (which may also allude to the Medici coat-of-arms), and the contemporary tower in the town wall of Vézelay built during the reign of Francis I. The reflection of this general type in Hunt's project – together with the presence of battlements, loopholes, and other massively Doric fortified details – might be seen simply as an ambitious reworking of Viollet-le-Duc's 'Fortress of Liberty' notion.[15] However, unlike the Serlian or Sangallesque examples, in Hunt's design the projecting headers not only are rock-faced and of unusually high relief, they occur only in every third course of masonry, forming a dilated, abstract pattern that finds its nearest historical parallel, strangely, in the Spanish Plateresque style in such picturesque examples of the late fifteenth century as the Infantado Palace in Guadalajara and the curious 'Casa de las Conchas' at Salamanca [94], where the bosses assume the form of scallop shells in allusion to the owner's title.[16]

Had Hunt been interested only in the 'Fortress of Liberty' notion, the structural, denser Franco-Italian type would have been more fitting than his apparent fusion of sources, in which, if anything, the Plateresque sense of pattern overshadows rugged structuralism. But if not exclusively evoking a 'Fortress of Liberty', to what else was Hunt so carefully alluding? Visually felicitous though his design may be, it seems unlikely that in the symbolically-charged project Hunt would have turned for a source to the obscure and historically isolated Plateresque were it not that the form could be invested with some appropriate meaning.

94. Casa de las Conchas, *c.* 1475. Salamanca

Like Bartholdi's Suez project that preceded it, the *Statue of Liberty* was intended to function not only as a symbolic light for mankind, but as a beacon for New York harbor (and to this extent it was not a pure monument).[17] The great prototype for lighthouses – an architectural genre, we recall, that summoned forth the fantasies of the 1852 competition – was one of the seven canonical wonders of the ancient world: the Pharos at Alexandria. All but destroyed by the fourteenth century, its original form was nevertheless available in summary and, of course, distorted form on ancient coins. In fact, the last illustration in that mine for eclectics, T. E. Donaldson's *Architectura Numismatica* of 1859, depicts just such a coin [95]. How else to reconstruct the double row of regularly

95. Pharos of Alexandria on an ancient coin

spaced projections but as that Plateresque rustication seen on Hunt's project (even though according to recent archaeological evidence they may have signified something else)?[18] If in fact Hunt had the entirely appropriate notion – for his time – to build the pedestal as the Pharos, the other major feature of the project would contribute to the allusion, for according to Quatremère de Quincy the Pharos had a 'gallery' (although it was probably more of a terrace).[19] Continuing in this vein to the logical end, it would not have been lost on Hunt that, as he knew from both ancient description and the coins, there had been a monumental statue crowning the Pharos. In the context of the *Liberty* project, where the statue, not its substructure, was to be the major feature, this knowledge would have brought to Hunt's mind that other canonical ancient wonder which Bartholdi (and practically everyone else, including Laboulaye and even Emma Lazarus) had in mind as the prototype of his harbor colossus, torch-holding, radiantly crowned and triumphant: the Colossus of Rhodes. In an age that produced such visions of eclecticism as, let us say, Thomas Cole's *The Course of Empire*, Professor C. R. Cockerell's 'The Professor's Dream',[20] or William Strickland's Tennessee State Capitol at Nashville (1846–59), crowned by an enlarged copy of the Lysicrates Monument in Athens, to what greater poetic heights could a scholarly architect like Hunt, perhaps somewhat frustrated with his humdrum fare of ordinary commissions after his splendid beginnings at the Louvre, aspire than to combine the Colossus of Rhodes with the Pharos of Alexandria?

Unfortunately, Hunt was not to build his visionary conception – probably the most appealing in appearance and symbolic conception of all his works. In 1884 dissatisfaction with its great height, which threatened to belittle the sculpture, together with a continuing, severe shortage of building funds, provoked a reduction in height (from 114 to 89 feet). Denied the tower-like massing, Hunt regretfully discarded the 'Pharos' project completely. He saw to it, however, that the reduction in size was financially fruitless: by com-

96. 'Pharos II' model.
R. M. Hunt,
1883-4

plicating the conformation of masonry Hunt managed to spend as much as had been estimated originally [97–102].[21]

The complication of forms in the definitive project served more than to compensate his pride. His first project made its great impression through sheer dimensions, broad splendor, and – to the initiate – its symbolic intent. Upon reflection, Hunt perceived in his conception a certain looseness that he came to regard as undesirable. Months before he was called upon to reduce and reshape the pedestal, he produced a second version of the 'Pharos' in which the major change – apart from the elimination of the 'Doric' frieze in the socle – was in the loggia [96]. Earlier it was set freely and with a certain iconic focus in the great rusticated wall, whereas now it became integrated with a massive new parapeted cornice that wraps itself around the entire shaft. In the ultimate project this process of complication and rationalization is carried to the point where intricately interlinked, densely involuted forms take the place of broad and free eclectic grandeur.

97A, B and C.
Pedestal projects for *Liberty*.
R. M. Hunt, 1884

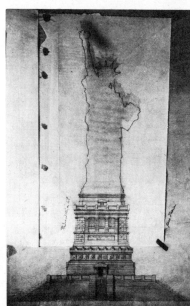
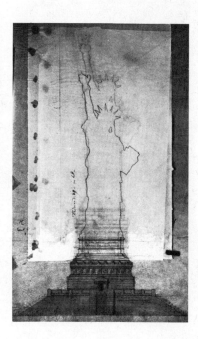

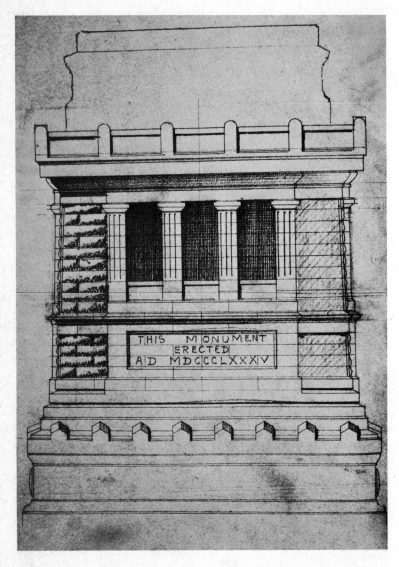

98. Pedestal project for *Liberty*.
R. M. Hunt, 1884.

It will be seen that this evolution of Hunt's ideas – and, looking back, Viollet-le-Duc's and Bartholdi's – within a single project is reminiscent of the fundamental transformation of late-eighteenth-century visionary architecture during the succeeding generations. The comprehension of just what was historically involved in such a parallelism – how, in fact, such a phenomenon was even possible –

99. Definitive pedestal project. R. M. Hunt, 7 August 1884

100 and 101. *Liberty*'s pedestal. R. M. Hunt, 1884-6

102. *Liberty*'s pedestal, detail.
R. M. Hunt, 1884-6

involves some account of the complex architectural currents in
Hunt's period. Stylistic survival and revival, reaction and progress
are always possibilities for the architect; in Hunt's age they were
particularly real alternatives, which accounts for much of its
extreme complexity and trendiness. At one basic level, however,
there remained two alternatives (although their outlines were often
blurred and even merged): the acceptance of the visionary Neo-
Classical ideal or its denial.

For just as the politics of nineteenth-century France were
haunted by the ghosts of revolutionary ideology, so too was it in
architecture. Beneath the architectural restorations of Baroque
and Renaissance styles and the waves of medieval revival there
was maintained not only the disciplined foundation of the great

tradition of French classicism, but something of the revolutionary ideology as well. Even if in compromised form, a severe classicist strain continued well into the mid-century in the work of prominent architects like Viollet-le-Duc and Labrouste, men who disdained the rising Second Empire Neo-Baroque and who would have exerted a counter-influence on Hunt during his years at the École (where the doctrine of Boullée and his pedagogic follower Durand would have been familiar lessons in any event). We have seen how all of *Liberty*'s architects revived the dormant revolutionary ideal of an *architecture parlante*.[22] But up through Hunt's first project they also drew on the manner conceived by the revolutionary architects to achieve that ideal (which the late Emil Kaufmann defined so well). Fundamental was a method of composition in distinct units, tending towards geometric purity, and the corresponding denial of the 'Renaissance-Baroque' system of interwoven, subordinated forms graded in shape, scale, and texture, expressing mechanical forces by organic elements. The revolutionary ideal posited new means to achieve coherence and life, especially through the emphatic contrast of geometry and textures, but also by the repetition of motifs at different heights on differing scale (Kaufmann's 'reverberation'). This revolutionary manner – often called Ledolcian after one of its two chief practitioners – was increasingly diluted in the nineteenth century by revitalized survival of the old 'Renaissance-Baroque' system and, especially after the mid-century, by picturesque elaboration in various eclectic modes.[23]

If Bartholdi's bold massing was the clearest reference to the geometry of the revolutionaries, their deployment of detail was most strongly present in Hunt's projects, where a powerful and extended Doric 'reverberation' runs between the sub-Doric portals, and from the Doric socle (the forty shields meant to carry the coats-of-arms of the forty states) to the triglyph-piers of the loggia and to the cornicework, whose moldings are not the common ones but an adaptation of the echinus-abacus sequence of the Doric

103. Design for
Washington Monument.
Arthur F. Mathews, 1879

capital. Yet even the first 'Pharos' project is less bold and disjunctive in its massing than the true revolutionary ideal, whose characteristically smooth, uninterrupted surfaces find themselves covered with an intricate texture here. The return to the pre-revolutionary system of binding ligatures occurs, we have seen, already in the 'Pharos' variation. When we reach the executed version the original revolutionary revival has been all but obscured by the true contemporary sensibility, which should have taken great delight in its ragged outline and density of internal complications and connections.

This taste is, for us, most interestingly embodied in American design in a project of 1879, when *Liberty* began to drift Hunt's way: Arthur F. Mathews' conception for a Washington Monument [103]. This widely published and highly praised (and seriously intended) Beaux-Arts extravaganza bears telling similarities in detail to Hunt – emphatic Doricism, battering, quoins, triple openings, terraces, embattled cresting (the surmounting figure even carries a torch). But that Hunt was conscious of the project is suggested less by his executed pedestal, where its seeming influence has been assimilated to the style of the 'Pharos' projects, than by one of his discarded ideas [104]. Here are exhibited Mathews' compound quoins (rusticated below, fluted above), two levels of triple center motif, and even the rusticated base above a Doric plinth, with a terminal cornice supported by closely spaced consoles. It seems, indeed, to be almost a simplified version of Mathews' idea, reduced to the status of a pedestal. Too much, however, should not be made of a dependence on Mathews, for there were ongoing French sources – especially Prix du Rome projects – on which both Americans probably depended.[24] Moreover, Hunt's pedestal, particularly as executed, does not unabashedly accept the full-blown Second Empire mode of Mathews (which is even mansarded), but maintains some Ledolcian restraint. In this way it is a design that in the mid-1880s may be observed as falling easily between, for example, Richardson's sublimely

104. Pedestal project for *Liberty*. R. M. Hunt, 1882–3

105. The Ames Monument.
H. H. Richardson, 1879

Egyptian Ames Monument in Wyoming of 1879 [105], and the brutalist fantasies of Bruno Schmitz of the 1890s towards which Hunt leads [48A and B].

But in the balance, although *Liberty*'s pedestal suggests revolutionary origins, it bears even more the scars of their defeat. Whereas in a true Ledolcian pedestal there would be a clear distinction of the parts of the elevation and an absolute tectonic integrity, Hunt takes pains now to introduce slippery transitions, most completely above the Doric frieze and battlements, where a series of graded setbacks leads uninterruptedly to the inscription plate. At this level an architectural inversion of great ingenuity begins. The inscription plate and loggia above stand forward from the rusticated quoins (that have replaced the original overall rustication), and this projection is continued in the partly broken cornice (a fully broken cornice would have been too sharp an accent for this scrupulous designer). Visually it is not the massive, rugged corners that provide the primary structure, as they traditionally and logically should. Instead the quoins are drained of strength, not merely by their recession, but also by the cutting of the huge blocks, which seem to form at each corner almost a loose pile (especially in contrast to the ashlar of the rest of the pedestal, and to the dense, identically scaled rustication of the fortress walls). The residual integrity of the corners is sapped by the sub-cornice that interrupts them at the line of the foot of the loggia. Thus undermined, the corners frame a continuous, emphatic flow of structure up the center of the elevation. But here the wall, which at the foot of the pedestal seems immensely thick and dense, is hollowed out, leaving the loggia a shadowy rear wall of uncertain depth and the relatively thin triglyph-piers. Above, the great cornice is so deeply undercut over the 'echinus' molding as to assume a certain illusion of floating, particularly out over the 'unsupported' corners. Thus, a sophisticated formal antagonism is generated between the dense solidity of the pedestal base, and the variously dematerialized main body above, with its loosely stacked, enormous quoins, its hollowed central structure, its huge floating cornice. Within the upper parts a high tension is created between the great scale and plasticity of the forms and their lack of visual density and weight.

This mannered play and inversion contradicts quite overtly the traditional, rationalist side of Hunt's training, in order to satisfy the jaded virtuoso streak of his own architectural age (which he had mastered at an early date under Lefuel in his work on the New Louvre in Paris, where, incidentally, one finds intricately rusticated quoins). But at the same time Hunt's pedestal achieves a controlled, rich and plastic composition that realizes the great scale of the site and the colossus, yet maintains the subordinate silhouette and posture of a pedestal. The very fragmentation that provides its architectural richness, and the draining of the structural density of the upper parts, combine to dissolve the great pedestal mass in favor of the statue, towards which the central stream of vertical energy runs, directing our eye in a subtle fashion away from itself and to Bartholdi's figure. The seeming irrationality of certain aspects of the design function in the context in a most subtly and successfully rational manner. No architect without Hunt's Parisian training

could have produced so masterly a composition, not only itself
fully realized, but at last perfectly joining and reconciling the
fortress and the colossus.[25] (And how well its architectural in-
tricacies befit the complexities of sculptural form and iconography.)

Probably no contemporary American architect could have fulfilled the commission better – with one exception: Henry Hobson
Richardson. It was he who not only had both the Parisian training
of Hunt and the genius that was denied him, but was the great
master of rusticated masonry that was *de rigueur* for a successful
pedestal on *Liberty*'s site. In fact, so extensive was Richardson's use
of rustication and so great was his renown by the early 1880s (the
last half-decade of his tragically short life) that even Hunt may have
been influenced by him. Such works as the Ames Monument, or
the Marshall Field Warehouse and the Pittsburgh Jail suggest that
had Richardson rather than Hunt received the commission for
Liberty's base, it would have far surpassed Hunt's design in boldness and power. Given the scale of the work one can well imagine
that a pedestal by Richardson would have been his most densely
powerful invention.[26]

As fate would have it, the *Liberty* commission nearly did descend
upon Richardson. One of the tangible achievements of Bartholdi's
initial trip to America in 1871 was meeting Richardson and receiving from him the commission for the large-scale sculptural
decoration of the bell-tower of the architect's first major success,
the Brattle Square Church in Boston.[27] Although Bartholdi did
finally deliver the huge reliefs, it was not until 1877, and by then
his relationship with Richardson seems to have gone sour. (The
architect also moved away from New York in 1874.) Much as one
regrets the lost opportunity for a grand Richardsonian design, it
was perhaps fitting that Richardson, who by the end of the 1870s
had developed far beyond his not quite mature state of 1871, should
have passed from the story of *Liberty*. The collaboration of Bartholdi and Hunt was in every respect appropriate. But Richardson
deserved better. His pedestal would have merited a Rodin.[28]

8. The Americans

Bartholdi's statue has become one of America's national shrines and, indeed, her only monumental image. Yet for all the men of consequence connected with its genesis, *Liberty*'s American patrons – who included William Evarts, John Jay, Richard Butler, and other prominent New Yorkers, and the prestigious Union League and Century Club – nearly failed to raise the funds for the pedestal that was the American part of the bargain.[1]

For a monument that was to become national property, the federal government seemed a natural contributor. However, it had been difficult even to persuade Congress in 1877 officially to accept the statue as a gift and provide a site for it. At the last moment, when the farce threatened to become an international disgrace, Congress did grudgingly provide funds for the unveiling ceremony' (excepting alcoholic refreshments) and for maintenance (as a lighthouse). But at the critical point in 1883 when the half-completed base was in financial peril, a bill providing $100,000 failed to pass the session, and only partly through the ineptitude of its supporters in letting it be attached as a rider to an unpopular and wholly unrelated proposal. The only official state support was the $50,000 appropriated by the legislature of New York State in 1884; but the vote was vetoed by Governor Cleveland, who two years later as President was proudly to take part in the unveiling ceremony.

Not surprisingly, the public was as ungenerous as its elected representatives. Extensive efforts had to be made to secure any private assistance whatsoever. From 1877 public appeals were made for donations. A promoter was engaged to travel around the

country to drum up support. An auction of donated objects of art
was held. Theatrical, musical and sporting benefit performances
were staged (including a 'monster entertainment' at the Casino
on Broadway). A poetry contest was held for publicity, which
Emma Lazarus reluctantly entered. The rich and influential were
importuned. Bartholdi contributed 200 signed models of the statue
and numerous personal appearances in 1876. The backers them-

106. Contribution certificate for the
pedestal fund, c. 1883

selves, many of them men of substance, were not ungenerous, and they appealed to their friends [106].

By early 1885 more than half of the estimated total expense of about $300,000 had been collected, not a small amount for the period, but disheartening. We have seen that the gift of the colossus was motivated by a unique set of political and cultural conditions in the ascendant French Third Republic. But there was no historical reason – beyond some vague Centennial sentiment – why a reciprocal spirit should have possessed the Americans (who after the Civil War, in any case, turned their increasing energies inward).[2] Nevertheless, the statue was quite a spectacular gift, and its tepid reception requires some explanation.

One factor not to be discounted – though it should not be overrated – was the cultural climate. To the European visitor, America, with the partial exception of a few eastern enclaves oriented towards the old European culture, seemed a land 'not particularly open to things of the imagination', as Bartholdi put it in a letter written during his grand tour of the country in 1871.[3] The European public of the period was naturally no less materially grasping than the citizens of the young republic, but their inheritance of the surviving accumulated efforts of several millennia gave them the illusion of a living cultural grandeur that greatly exaggerated the true energies which they allotted for authentic artistic creation. Yet the great inheritance, and the lack of one across the Atlantic, did (and still does) condition attitudes towards urban and architectural design and monument building.

More specifically, America had little experience of the wave of monument building which had afflicted nineteenth-century Europe. As of 1875–85 heroic statuary was rare, not to speak of colossi. The conditioned positive reaction of Europeans to projects for commemorative monuments was absent.[4] There should, in fact, be little wonder that Bartholdi's visionary statue – said to be a gift, which made it seem even less probable – met not only a generally tepid response, but downright skepticism. When the arm was exhibited in 1876, the sanity of its creator was doubted – his having, apparently, started from the top down without knowing what he would do next. This whimsical vein of comment – which found a touching expression in the proto-Oldenburgian suggestion to immerse the statue upside down in the Central Park Reservoir, 'as if drowned'[5] – seems to have been only half in jest, and to have reflected a more deep-lying disdain and hostility (not to mention the objection of the Catholic press to the 'pagan goddess' of libertarian values).[6] American artists – whatever their motives and however sound their judgment – were not overly appreciative of *Liberty*'s formal qualities. To one now obscure sculptor (Launt Thompson) she seemed to be set up falsely, the weight on the wrong leg, the arm out of line, etc. Another critic objected (not without cause [65]) that from the Battery the statue resembled 'a bag of potatoes with a stick projecting from it'.[7] New York's wealthy class of art patrons, it was said, considered the statue to be an unsound aesthetic investment ('not a work of art').[8] The even more pragmatic imagination dwelt on the dubiousness of a gift statue which had to be ransomed, in effect, by erecting a pedestal of equal, if not greater expense. There may even have been half-conscious suspicions of the kind the citizens of Troy entertained before they took in that giant, hollow statue of a horse: unsolicited gifts from strangers are not the most welcome (particularly when those strangers only a decade earlier had flirted with the Confederacy and threatened to annex Mexico).

The most abiding misunderstanding was that the gift was not so much to the nation, but to New York. Thus, it was generally felt that, if anyone, the residents of New York should pay. When they balked, the newspapers of several cities – including Milwaukee, Boston, and particularly Philadelphia, home of the Liberty Bell and where the arm was first exhibited – seriously proposed that the site be transferred to their more deserving city, whose patriotic citizens would immediately put up the funds. This kind of empty banter, encouraged by Bartholdi during his visit of 1876, may have had a healthy competitive effect on New York emotionally;[9] but financially, by 1884-5 the impulse was played out. In New York the ordinary citizen continued to feel the statue to be a rich man's folly, and rich men could pay. But the monied class – who in fact at the time had abandoned themselves not only to profligate luxury, but to an orgy of importation of European artifacts, even architecture – declined the responsibility. The great wealth was mostly new, and the possessors hard-headed capitalists: the monument, even if French, was perhaps of too populist a sentiment. For them *Liberty* was unwelcome in the United States for much the same reasons that it was exported from Paris.

Things could have dragged along for years this way. It might all have come to nought, the components of Bartholdi's statue moldering away for years in their two-hundred-odd shipping cases – had it not been for the timely intervention of Joseph Pulitzer. Immigrating from Hungary in 1864 to participate in the Civil War, by the early 1880s he had worked his way to great power in American journalism, pioneering in the so-called 'yellow press', transforming the newspaper into a true mass medium of the working classes. Pulitzer had taken an early interest in the *Statue of Liberty*. His motives were, of course, mixed. In part, it was a sentimental cause. But Pulitzer's sure instinct told him there was sensation in the story, and any publicity was good publicity, especially for the New York *World*, which he took over in 1883.

By the critical spring of 1885 Pulitzer realized that the early tactic of a simple appeal to the public – such as he himself had offered two years previously – would now be insufficient. An intensive campaign was necessary (and was now made possible by the enormous increase in the circulation of the *World*). It began with broadside blasts of criticism of the rich, any number of whom, it was pointed out, could easily have written a check for the entire amount. This kind of recrimination continued through the *World* campaign and was directed at the less affluent classes as well, evoking a sense of shame at the lack of generosity towards America's French friends and the 'noble' sculptor. Other newspapers, including Pulitzer's own St Louis *Post-Dispatch*, were enlisted (although the other New York papers uniformly abused the campaign). Continuing progress reports were published, stressing the project's formal and material grandeur (even *bigger* than the Brooklyn Bridge towers and the Tribune Tower). Its symbolism was hammered home, particularly the fact that the statue was meant not just for New York, but for all America. Indeed, it was the Pulitzer campaign that first dispelled the popular misconception about the proprietorship of *Liberty* and began to plant her emotional roots in the mainland.

But the financial success of the campaign was due most of all to an ingenious, if simple promotional device. Anonymous acts of charity may be the noblest, but Pulitzer, who understood so well the ways of mass motivation, published daily the names and amounts of every donation, however small. This gave rise to the myth that school children paid for the base. Young and old, there were finally 121,000 donors, largely from New York but a good number from outside (one as far as Texas), who by August 1885 – less than five months after the campaign began – contributed the $100,000 immediately needed (and eventually a considerable amount more towards the finishing touches). So much in fact was raised that $1000 was available for an extravagant Tiffany silver-work trophy given to Bartholdi shortly before he returned to France, with an inscription expressing the gratitude of Pulitzer's army [107].

In the end, everybody finally joined in acclamation of the *Statue of Liberty* (or at least refrained from cavil). Members of New York society fell over one another to participate in the dedication ceremonies at Bedloe's Island on 28 October 1886, from which the public that had sponsored the construction was naturally excluded, although allowed to watch from the shore. All the world seemed to be there – certainly all New York, which had boisterously accompanied the colorful parade down to preliminary ceremonies

107. *Liberty* trophy.
J. H. Whitehouse for Tiffany & Co.,
1886

at City Hall and the Battery, for it was a day to remember [108]. On the island speech after speech was heard in the rain – but not that of Senator Evarts addressing the President. For, before he had finished, Bartholdi, responding to a false cue, unveiled the face of his goddess and triggered off a chorus of foghorns and a twenty-one-gun salute [1]. The sculptor, lionized already on his visit of 1876, was the man of the hour – it was officially, in fact, 'Bartholdi Day' ('You are the greatest man in America today!' said President Cleveland).[10] Given golden keys to the city and later fêted at Delmonico's by all the notables, it was his proudest moment. He could consider himself fortunate; his only regret was that his aged mother could not be alongside him, and that Laboulaye, who had led him to the vision of the promised land, could not join him there, having died at a ripe age in 1883.

But soon all *Liberty*'s creators were to pass from the scene, like ripples in water spreading from the center of a disturbance and subsiding. Several decades passed, and the old historical realities were displaced by new. Like an adopted child, the statue retained the hereditary physical form of its natural parents, but took its mature character from its foster home. The gesture and diffuse collection of attributes of the statue received much of their meaning from the historical context. When this was gone, the political allusion intended by Laboulaye and his colleagues was largely lost (not to mention the more shadowy, personal meaning it had for Bartholdi). For the Americans, there was no profit in maintaining the symbolism of international revolution (even on the intended moderate terms of the 'conservative republicans'). Few among the American public wished to be reminded of the frailty of the thirteen colonies in 1776, and how they had welcomed aid from a mighty nation that had since grown soft. And certainly whatever was sensed of the imperialist French undertones of the statue was felt as abhorrent. The purging of cumbersome allusion has been observed in the eventual shift of the statue's popular name: at the time of its appearance often called 'the Bartholdi

108. Fireworks at the dedication of *Liberty*, 1886

statue', *Liberty Enlightening the World* became simply *The Statue of Liberty*, the embodiment of the universal ideal in a particular work instead of the old incorporeal image. But this neutralization of meaning was equally valid for all the world. Had it been the only transformation of meaning *Liberty* would have been a statue without a country, as it were, and would have involved no special significance for the United States. What came to pass, however, was that *Liberty* acquired, simultaneously with her becoming a new universal icon, a close identification with her home, for she was not only neutralized, but naturalized as well. She gradually assumed something of deep American appeal.

As early as 1883 the French meanings were lost on Emma Lazarus. In her famous poem 'The New Colossus', the beacon of liberty seen across the sea was not intended to serve France or any other nation, but rather to guide those Europeans eager for a new life *away* from Europe entirely, to the 'golden door' of America, where an uplifted torch was symbolic not of 'enlightenment' but simply of 'welcome'.[11] Most Americans today are far removed from their immigrant ancestors' state of mind, so many of whom *were*, to one degree or another, Lazarus's 'wretched refuse', particularly during the closing decades of the nineteenth century and the early years of the twentieth [54]. Moreover, most travelers now come to the country not by ship, but by airplane. The sentiment that the statue carried for the millions of European immigrants who arrived before the 'golden door' all but closed in the 1920s has dwindled, although surviving as a pervasive folkloric theme. But in 1903, at the height of immigration, this sentiment was so widely accepted as expressing the statue's meaning that a plaque bearing the poem was affixed to the pedestal as an *ex post facto* inscription.[12]

The experience of the immigrants involved crucial implications for *Liberty*. Their vision of America as political and economic liberation reinforced a natural tendency to perceive *Liberty* 'welcoming' as 'America welcoming'. The statue was becoming the image not so much of America the protagonist of Liberty, but simply America itself.

This new identity was facilitated by the absence of competitors. Of course, Liberty, early identified with America, became a catchword of the new American republic. But as a personification of America it was by no means alone, or even the first. An Indian Princess, deriving from Renaissance 'Allegories of the Four Continents', was the earliest. She was later transformed, during the Revolutionary era, into a plumed Greek Goddess, Hercules and Minerva also being associated with America at this time. Finally there arrived the indigenous characters of Brother Jonathan and Uncle Sam who survived in vernacular iconography while most of the other figures soon fell from fashion. As the nineteenth century drew on to Bartholdi's day, it becomes clear that *Liberty* had only one true competitor as the American icon – Columbia. This figure was a vaguely defined, synthetic personage whose name derived from Columbus. Its use is first recorded in the 1690s and it became increasingly popular after the Revolution – *Hail Columbia* (1798), Joel Barlow's *Columbiad* (1807). But Bartholdi – by choosing Liberty – effectively pre-empted a monumental realization of Columbia. For his statue subsumed Columbia's vague image as a grand lady in white. Thus, in the end, there could be no successful competitor to Bartholdi's personification of a principal American idea.[13]

The tide of immigration subsided, and at the same time the new American image was diffused deeply into the national consciousness. Its force was carried considerably by the immigrants. But it was during the Great War of 1914–18 that the statue attained potent meaning for all American groups. Ships that had brought the diverse immigrant masses 'welcomed' by *Liberty* now sailed out under her militant gaze carrying united, armed Americans [110]. 'Make the world safe for democracy' was now the cry, and 'Liberty bonds' one of the means [109]. Emma Lazarus's poem had been isolationist in sentiment: 'Liberty' had withdrawn into America and become one with her. When the statue, with her new lighting of

1916,[14] turned to face the world again (and this time not just France) it was as America, Light of the World – America, not only as the embodiment of liberty, but as a land which had become a symbol itself and less of a refuge for the world's 'wretched refuse' against

LAND OF THE FREE AND
HOME OF THE BRAVE

110 (*left*). First World War poster

111. First World War poster.
By J. Pennell

THAT LIBERTY SHALL NOT
PERISH FROM THE EARTH
BUY LIBERTY BONDS
FOURTH   LIBERTY   LOAN

whom a wall of restrictions was being raised. Bartholdi's name for his statue – indeed, even its new abbreviated, universalist popular title – was now a euphemism: what he had unwittingly wrought was the Statue of America [110–12].

In retrospect, now, it is possible to reconsider the factors that have granted *Liberty* such longevity and unrivalled celebrity. In our

112. *Liberty* from a helicopter

time, what seems to be a deep human urge to allegorical expression – especially at the collective level – has not been rooted out by modernism, but only suppressed. As the greatest survival in the West of the tradition of allegorical personification, *Liberty* has been a recipient of this bottled-up energy. But, obviously, her awesome potency as a symbol is also due to what she has come to symbolize: the richest and mightiest nation on earth, and the one traditionally believed to have a special destiny in the liberation and realization of the spirit of man. It is a belief not always in harmony with the turn of events, but it is an abiding idea, and channels a tremendous force to *Liberty* as allegorical survival.

Liberty's vitality centers on her personification of America, but it also involves her extraordinary fluidity as a symbolic image. The statue's definitive symbolism was not exclusive. It dimmed, but it did not extinguish the earlier 'French' and 'immigrant' meanings. The statue still, in fact, thrives as Bartholdi's Goddess of Liberty and as Lazarus' 'Mother of Exiles' (the latter role now aggrandized in the Museum of American Immigration at the statue's feet). Yet *Liberty*'s variability of meaning comprehends not only the persistence of her iconographic history, but also an ongoing relationship to manifold aspects of actuality. Such a famous symbol begs reinterpretation, and *Liberty* has proved to be a Protean source of public imagery. This has been much abetted by her site, posture, expression, and especially her attributes, which are open to seemingly unlimited possibilities of reinterpretation through changes of every conceivable kind – exaggeration and distortion, deletion and supplementation, fragmentation and duplication. Particularly common is the process of abbreviation (already by, and for, Bartholdi [70, 71, 107]) in which the mere presence of the torch or radiant crown suffices to establish as *Liberty* an allegory that may range from the outrageous to the banal, or from the sublime to the simply vulgar.

But the reinterpretations and uses of the *Statue of Liberty* have been so numerous and various as to defy compilation. Even before the statue was completed it was worked into popular iconography

113. From *Harper's Weekly*,
2 April 1881. T. Nast

for private gain (for example, as the masthead for Pulitzer's *The World*), and it appeared as sensationalist allegory, most notably in Thomas Nast's grisly 1881 woodcut protesting a witches' brew of crime, epidemics, and political corruption [113].[15] It has since been the subject of every conceivable commercial and ideological exploitation, among which its use as a head-piece for wigs in advertising copy, or with tears streaming at some political outrage, represent the average level of imagination (although there has been some comic relief in this process, notably Claes Oldenburg's 'project' for the total substitution of a giant electric fan).[16] *Liberty*

114. *Planet of the Apes*, final shot, 1967

has naturally appeared – even 'starred' – in the cinema: as a heroine in Hitchcock's memorable *Saboteur* of 1942[17] – a time when *Liberty*'s lights were extinguished to make the same point as when they went on in 1916; as the universally understood means of the 'shattering' revelation of nuclear holocaust at the end of the science-fiction spectacular, *Planet of the Apes*, 1967 [114]; or, in a more crassly exploitative way [115], in a dismal Hollywood product starring a rejuvenated, septuagenarian Mae West posing in advertisements in the statue's guise (referring also to a famous studio that has adopted a disguised *Liberty* as *its* symbol). This latter

115. Film advertisement, 1970   116. Satirical revue poster, New York, 1973

tendency, which seems to be intensifying of late (perhaps a collective expression of the degraded state of American morale [116]),[18] was practiced by Bartholdi himself, who patented the form of *Liberty* in 1876 in hopes of ultimately being able to compensate financially his years of unpaid labor with royalties from copies, a scheme that came to practically nothing because of a faulty contract in which the inattentive sculptor signed away his legal rights to a shady manufacturer.[19]

Perhaps the most unthinking attempt to exploit the statue has been by the feminist movement, which was drawn towards *Liberty* at an early date.[20] The most recent factions have tended to make of the statue a symbol of woman 'liberated' and a firebrand of feminist revolution. The irony is, of course, that in the feminist context she is as much martyr as heroine, for she stands immobilized and most heavily draped – like any presentable lady of the nineteenth century – idealized on a high pedestal and put there by a whole crew of firm believers in the traditional arrangement between the sexes. Furthermore, not as we see her, but as we know her, this decent woman takes on an altogether different character – for a fee she is open to all for entry and exploration from below.

Despite iconographic assault and degradation Bartholdi's colossus remains, for good or ill, the image of America. As such the question of its meaning has been truly deepened, to my knowledge, only by – of all writers – Franz Kafka. The opening paragraph of one of his major novels, *Amerika*, written in 1913, depicts the protagonist, a poor immigrant boy, standing 'on the liner slowly entering the harbor of New York, [when] a sudden burst of sunshine seemed to illumine the *Statue of Liberty*, so that he saw it in a new light, although he had sighted it long before. The arm with the sword rose up as if newly stretched aloft, and round the figure blew the free winds of heaven. "So high," he said to himself . . .' Kafka may have been thinking of the upraised sword of the *Arminius*. But even in faraway Prague, he was not one senselessly or unwittingly to confuse such things (and such phrases as 'saw it in a new light' and especially 'as if newly stretched aloft' hint that he knew what he was about). The matter-of-fact tone in which the misrepresentation is expressed is entirely characteristic of Kafka, whose supreme importance as a writer lies in the haunting, final truth of his nightmare world. It seems neither melodramatic nor out of place to note that now there is every reason to believe that the resolution of the question – whose image of America is real, Bartholdi's or Kafka's? – could touch the fate of the world.

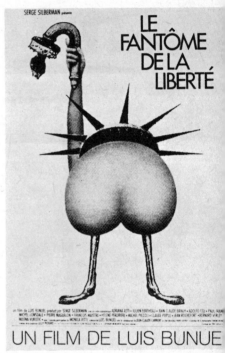

SERGE SILBERMAN présente

LE FANTÔME DE LA LIBERTÉ

UN FILM DE LUIS BUNUE

117. Film advertisement, 1974

Notes

INTRODUCTION (*pages 15-19*)

1. E. H. Gombrich, 'The Use of Art for the Study of Symbols', *American Psychologist*, xx (1965) 33 ff. (reprinted in *Probleme der Kunstwissenschaft*, II [1966], 11 ff.).

I. THE CIRCUMSTANCES (*pages 21-40*)

1. The image of generosity and flowing good will of Bartholdi and his French compatriots dominates the popular literature on the *Statue of Liberty*, such as B. Levine and I. F. Story, *Statue of Liberty* (National Park Service Historical Handbook Series No. 11) (Washington, 1961); W. Price, *Bartholdi and the Statue of Liberty* (Chicago, 1959) (an intelligent book for the juvenile audience); and O. Handlin, *Statue of Liberty* (New York, 1971) (well-illustrated, with emphasis on historical background and especially on immigration). The story is accepted even in more scholarly works, such as J. Betz's excellent biography of Bartholdi (Paris, 1954) and A. Gschaedler's *True Light on the Statue of Liberty and Its Creator* (Narbeth, Pennsylvania, 1966), generally a well-documented work of original research (but with little on artistic or political aspects). Similarly limited are the extensively researched government reports on the statue (MSS. on deposit at the National Park Service office in New York), R. M. Hughes, *The French Story*, and J. Holliman, *The American Story* (the latter more solid). H. Pauli and E. B. Ashton, *I Lift My Lamp, The Way of a Symbol* (New York, 1958), puts *Liberty* in her immediate political context, making several of the points found in this chapter, without, however, dealing with personalities or artistic questions in any depth. A good balance is struck by R. McKenny and E. Bransten, 'Colossus', *New York* (supplement of New York *Herald Tribune* Sunday edition), 24 October 1965, 14 ff. (with the journalistic virtue of liveliness, and the vice of willful distortion).

2. On Bartholdi, Betz, op. cit.; Gschaedler, op. cit.; S. Lami, *Dictionnaire des sculpteurs de l'école française au dix-neuvième siècle* (Paris, 1914-21).

3. The circle included Henri Martin, the prominent historian; the Comte de Rémusat, a liberal political figure and writer, husband of the grand-daughter of Lafayette whose grandson Oscar was also included; and, among others, such well known names as Wolowski, de Gasparin, Jules de Lasteyrie and de Tocqueville's heir.

4. French history throughout this book is standard. An accessible and excellent survey is A. Cobban, *A History of Modern France* (Harmondsworth, 1965). Cf. also, G. P. Gooch, *The Second Empire* (London, 1960), and G. Chapman, *The Third Republic of France, The First Phase, 1871-91* (London, 1962).

5. For Laboulaye biography, cf. *Bluntschli, Lieber, and Laboulaye*, ed. D. C. Gilman (Baltimore, 1884); H. Wallon, *Laboulaye* (Paris, 1889). When elected to the National Assembly in 1871, he was made chairman of the Committee for the Reorganization of Public Instruction in France.

6. *La République constitutionelle* (Paris, 1871), 1.

7. On this technique, W. R. West, *Contemporary French Opinion on the American Civil War* (Baltimore, 1924), 14 ff.; L. M. Case and W. F. Spencer, *The U.S. and France, Civil War Diplomacy* (Philadelphia, 1970), 604 ff. and *passim*. On art, D. D. Egbert, *Social Radicalism and the Arts, Western Europe* (New York, 1970), 164 ff.

8. Gooch, op. cit., 28.

9. Cf. Handlin, op. cit., 32 ff., 68 ff.

10. *Histoire des États-Unis* (Paris, 1855-66); *Paris in America*, tr. Mary Booth (New York, 1963) (orig. ed. 1863).

11. *The United States and France* (Boston, 1862), 13 (originally appeared in the *Journal des Débats*, 26-7 August 1862).

12. F. A. Bartholdi, *The Statue of Liberty Enlightening the World, described by the Sculptor Bartholdi*, ed. A. T. Rice (New York, 1885).

13. Salon of 1866, N. 2627. Pauli and Ashton (op. cit.) speculate that Laboulaye wanted Bartholdi to help him win office in the Assembly as Alsatian representative.

14. On the French reaction to the Civil War and the death of Lincoln, Case and Spencer, op. cit., 571 ff., 587 f., 604 ff.

15. Henri Martin was a charter member of the salon (1864 ff.) of Mme Adam (Juliette Lamberte) – 'La Grande Française' – the most influential political salon since Mme de Staël's and where the rural Gambetta was 'civilized' (Gooch, op. cit., 274 ff.; on the *affaire Baudin*, 267 ff.). On the difficulties of artistic expression of the opposition under the Second Empire (and its persistence), n. 7 above and A. Boime, 'Thomas Couture and the Evolution of Painting in Nineteenth-Century France', *Art Bulletin*, LI (1969), 53 n. 64.

16. *La République constitutionelle* (Paris, 1871), 7.

17. Gschaedler, op. cit., 14.

18. ibid., 20.

19. Betz, op. cit., 98. Bartholdi remarks that it seems 'a good time to realize the voyage of which we spoke', asks for letters of introduction, speaks of his hopes to work out several important projects, but states that he 'hope[s] above all to realize my project for a monument in honor of Independence,' adding, 'I have relied and I still rely on your works on this subject . . .'

20. ibid., 101 ff.; Gschaedler, op. cit., 23 ff.

21. *Discours populaires* (Paris, 1869), 36.

22. Bartholdi, op. cit., 24.

23. Hughes and Holliman, op. cit., *passim*; Gschaedler, op. cit., 36 ff.

24. F. Farre, ed., *Union Franco-Américaine, Discours de MM. Henri Martin, E. B. Washburne, Édouard Laboulaye et J. W. Forney, prononcés au banquet du 6 Novembre 1875* (Paris, 1875).

25. 'Toute idée appelle un symbole. Ce symbole, M. Bartholdi l'a trouvé . . . C'est lui qui a eu l'idée d'ériger ce colosse, et quoique je ne sois pas artiste, je crois pouvoir dire, sans me tromper, qu'il y a là une grande idée . . .' (Farre [ed.], op. cit., 37).

26. 'Dieu liberté' was also the motto of *L'Avenir*, the short-lived organ of Catholic liberalism founded in 1830.

27. Cf. Gooch, op. cit., *passim.*, for the importance of liberty as an issue at the time. Louis Napoleon tried to win over Victor Hugo in 1848 with such statements as 'I stand for Liberty'; later the 'betrayed' Hugo wrote his long *Napoléon le Petit* – calling him 'the nocturnal garroter of liberty'. In a letter of 1853, Flaubert, who detested contemporary France (and politics in general), wrote, 'Our dear country detests liberty . . . that is why I love art: there, at any rate, is liberty, in the realm of the imagination.' (Gooch, op. cit., 282, 297).

28. The benefit performance of Gounod's canata 'La Liberté éclairant le monde' took place 25 April 1876 at the New Opera of Paris; it was poorly attended and raised only 8000 Francs. Lyrics were by Émile Guiard (full text of the hymn in Hughes, op. cit., 26 f.).

29. The replica was a gift of the American residents of Paris; it was presented to the city in May 1885 at the Place des États-Unis; in 1889 it was moved to the permanent site on the Île des Cygnes (Gschaedler, op. cit., 97 f.; Hughes, op. cit., 44 f., 49).

30. Although financial support for *Liberty* was widespread – including contributions from 181 towns and over 100,000 individuals by 1881 – the bulk of the *c.* $400,000 spent by the French came from solid citizens – especially businessmen with American markets – center-left groups, and, interestingly enough, Masonic Lodges of which Henry Martin was the Grand Master. Freemasons had been connected with such pro-American sentiments since the Revolutionary period, when the idea of America as a potential Utopia was strong among them, and when the Lodge of the Nine Sisters in Paris was a meeting place of American and French philosophers of Enlightenment. But French Freemasonry tended, if anything, to be more radical than Laboulaye's party. Although it supported the Republic (and *Liberty*), with many prominent leaders among its members, there was no particular political connection or 'plot' (J. A. Faucher and A. Ricker, *Histoire de la Franc-Maçonnerie en France* [Paris, 1967] 324 ff.). It is suggestive that Bartholdi's initiation into the Alsace-Lorraine Lodge of Paris occurred on 4 October 1875 (ibid., 358), just a month prior to the 6 November *Liberty* banquet – conceivably to further patronage for his project, but perhaps purely coincidental. Cf. Pauli and Ashton, op. cit., 142 ff.; Hughes, op. cit.; Gschaedler, op. cit., 63 f. On French-American relationships in the period, n. 7 above, and also T. A. Bailey, *A Diplomatic History of the American People* (New York, 1946).

31. Paradoxically, *Liberty* might also be viewed as expressing the strong current of *anti*-colonialism of the 1870s – as colonies liberated, a projection onto Great Britain of internal French problems (cf. S. H. Roberts, *The History of French Colonial Policy* [London, 1929]; after the loss of Alsace-Lorraine, the colonies were seen as dissipation of energies needed to build up France internally and recover lost national soil, generating a fierce controversy that came to a peak around 1880, after which colonialism more or less won out under Jules Ferry).

32. One critic deemed the statue 'a messenger of concord, liberty, civilization, and peace . . . that speaks of France, French art, and the French soul' (A. Michel in *Revue alsacienne*, July 1884 [cited by Betz, op. cit., 170 f.]). At the ceremony of completion of the same year [77], Jules Grevy, French President, exclaimed that Liberty 'will magnify France beyond the seas' (Gschaedler, op. cit., 82).

33. There is one final circumstance not to be discounted here in allowing for *Liberty*'s origins in France of the late 1860s and 1870s. Nothing of the motivation for *Liberty*, or her purposes, all highly symbolic in nature, would probably have had much effect, nor would have been intended, had not France, particularly after 1870, been in a less than hypersensitive emotional state (the soft core of the stiff official posture). It seems that in those years growing religious zeal fused with profound disorder, economic stress, and a malaise and guilt stemming from a humiliating war and the horrors of the Commune. The miracle of Lourdes occurred in 1858, but it was in the early 1870s that mass pilgrimages by rail were organized. France, in hope of salvation, consecrated herself to the Sacred Heart of Jesus; the church of the Sacre Coeur crowning Montmartre was begun in 1873. And this hypersensitivity towards symbols is manifest in the destruction of Napoleon's Vendôme column by the Commune and, above all, in the fate of the comte de Chambord, refusing the crown of France for which he had thirsted his whole life for the sake of a banner – and France, refusing for the same reason the king she longed for.

2. BARTHOLDI (*pages 41-61*)

1. R. Mirolli, 'Monuments for the Middle Class', *Nineteenth Century French Sculpture*, J. B. Speed Art Museum, November 1971 (Louisville, 1971), 16. L. Hautecoeur, *Histoire de l'architecture classique en France*, VII (Paris, 1957), 106 ff., notes in connection with Bartholdi's *Liberty* that in the 1880s, 'Dans toutes les provinces, des rues, des avenues, des places, des statues de la République manifestèrant l'attachement des Français à l'ordre nouveau.'

2. For Bartholdi's training, Betz, op. cit., 21 ff. On Scheffer, S. Giedion, *Architektur und Gemeinschaft* (Hamburg, 1956), tr. as *Architecture, You and Me* (Cambridge, 1958), 15 ff.

3. Betz, op. cit., 238 ff.

4. R. Goldwater and M. Treves, *Artists on Art* (New York, 1945), 155. On mid-nineteenth-century academic ideology, A. Boime, *The Academy and French Painting in the Nineteenth Century* (London, 1971); J. C. Sloane, *French Painting between the Past and the Present* (Princeton, 1950).

5. F. Licht, *Sculpture, 19th and 20th Centuries* (Greenwich, Conn., 1967), is very articulate on this aspect of nineteenth-century sculpture. See also, Sloane, op. cit.; Mirolli, op. cit.; A. Boime, 'The Second Republic's Contest for the Figure of the Republic', *Art Bulletin*, LIII (1971), 68 ff.; F. Novotny, *Painting and Sculpture in Europe, 1780 to 1880* (Harmondsworth and Baltimore, 1960), 220 ff.; and *The Academy*, ed. T. B. Hess and J. Ashbery (*Art News Annual*, XXXIII [1967]).

6. Modern literature on monuments is weak, but advancing. See the entry in the McGraw-Hill *Encyclopedia of World Art* for a conscientious survey with bibliography. Giedion, op. cit., 25 ff., offers a singular perspective on monuments and contemporary culture. For a searching study of the sculptural monument in antiquity see P. Fehl, *The Classical Monument* (New York, 1972). Rewarding reading (in addition to material cited elsewhere) on monuments of the French Revolutionary period and the nineteenth century includes: A. Neumeyer, 'Monuments to "Genius" in German Classicism', *Journal of the Warburg Institute*, II (1938-9), 159 ff.; R. L. Alexander, 'The Public Memorial and Godefroy's Battle Monument', *Journal of the Society of Architectural Historians*, XVII, 1 (March 1958), 19 ff.; R. Zeitler, *Die Kunst des 19. Jahrhunderts* (Berlin, 1966), *passim*; J. del Caso, 'Sculpture et Monument dans l'art français à l'époque néo-classique', *Stil und Überlieferung in der Kunst des Abendlandes, Akten des 21. Internationalen Kongresses für Kunstgeschichte in Bonn 1964* (Bonn, 1966), I, 190 ff.; Mirolli, op. cit., 9 ff.; H. J. Hansen, ed., *Late Nineteenth Century Art* (New York, 1972), tr. M. Bullock; P. Ferriday, 'Free standing and civic', *Studio International*, CLXXXIV (July/Aug. 1972), 41 ff.; and the impressive recent collection of articles on the German-speaking countries, *Denkmäler im 19. Jahrhundert*, ed. H.-E. Mittig and V. Plagemann (Munich, 1972). A less searching but more comprehensive French counterpart to the last mentioned is M. Rheims, *La Sculpture au XIX Siècle* (Paris, 1972). For an impressive collection of illustrations, esp. of German monuments, Verlag E. Wasmuth, *Monumente und Standbilder Europas* (Berlin, 1914).

7. G. Pauli, *Die Kunst des Klassizismus und der Romantik* (Berlin, 1925), 68 f. (in general out of date, but good on this point). On the 'sublime' in the Neo-Classic period, H. Honour, *Neo-Classicism* (Harmondsworth, 1968), 141 ff.; on its survival through the nineteenth century, R. Rosenblum,

Modern Painting and the Northern Romantic Tradition: Friedrich to Rothko (New York, London, 1974).

8. Betz, op. cit., 29, 37 ff.

9. Bartholdi, op. cit., 38.

10. ibid., 36.

11. Between the *General Rapp* of 1855 and the *Liberty* and Belfort *Lion* of 1871 onwards (the *Lion* executed 1875-80), Bartholdi worked almost continuously on large-scale projects: 1858, project for a fountain in Bordeaux (won competition, but never executed); 1859, project for the Palais du Longchamp at Marseilles (with charges of plagiarism against Espérandieu, the eventual builder, ending in bitter litigation); 1858-64, fountain in Avalon; 1863-4, *Bruat* fountain, Colmar; 1867-9, Egyptian projects (see below); 1869, *Vercingétorix* projected on huge scale for Clermont-Ferrand (25-35 meters in height), executed at 6 meters in 1903. Bartholdi's rising renown came in tangible form as a membership in the Légion d'Honneur, including the rank of Chevalier at the unveiling of the Bruat monument in Colmar in 1864 (which included a choral work singing his praises; Betz, op. cit., 56).

12. On the controversial figure of Ismail, cf. E. DeLeon, *The Khedive's Egypt* (London, 1879), noting his 1867 Paris visit to the Anti-Slavery Societies of France and England, of which Laboulaye was the president, and his statement (another occasion) 'Every man is mad on some subject. My mania is building' (166 f., 175); D. Douen, *Histoire du Règne du Khédive Ismail* (Rome, 1934), describing his 1867 and 1869 Paris visits in detail; P. Crabitès, *Ismail the Maligned Khedive* (London, 1933), with a discussion of the eventual engineer of *Liberty*'s pedestal, Charles P. Stone, his chief of staff 1870 ff., and noting that Ismail actually did build fifteen lighthouses at a cost of $138,000 (94 ff.).

13. Theme identified in a letter to the London *Times*, 10 October 1904 (cited by Hughes, op. cit., 68); cf. Gschaedler, 12 ff. According to the scale engraved on the side of the 1867 maquette, the statue was to be *c.* 19.5 meters to the head, or *c.* 28 meters to the torch (*Liberty* is 46); and the pedestal *c.* 15 meters in height.

14. Published by César Daly in his *Revue générale de l'architecture*, 1852. My thanks to David Van Zanten for this reference, and for evidence that the 'Lequeu' tradition continued into the nineteenth century, with representatives in every generation in 'progressive' circles that Bartholdi was in contact with. The central figure around mid-century was Labrouste, whose atelier he frequented (Betz, op. cit., 24) and

who, for example, had proposed a colossal shield in the competition for a monument to Napoleon of 1841 (*R.G.A.*, II [1841] Pl. 32). Etex, with whom Bartholdi studied, was also connected with this tradition. Cf. also Danjoy's Demidoff tomb of 1850 in the Cimetière de l'Est in the form of a Russian funeral pyre (C. Daly, *Architecture funéraire contemporaine* [Paris, 1871], 2 Sect [D¹], 'La Foi, La Mort et la Glorification', Pl. 12 f.), and, in an earlier generation, the notions of Dédeban (e.g. L. Hautecoeur, *Histoire de l'architecture classique en France* [Paris, 1955], VI, 188). Symbolic lighthouse projects continue into the twentieth century: Antonio Sant'Elia's lighthouse project of 1914 was adopted in Como in 1933 as a *Monument to the Fallen*. The great real lighthouse of the nineteenth century was the Eddystone Lighthouse, constructed on an exposed ocean outcropping off the coast of England, 1878-90, where four lighthouses had been destroyed by wave action in the previous 200 years.

15. On the 1848 projects see Boime, op. cit., p. 80. Gombrich, op. cit., emphasizes *Liberty*'s natural, rather than arbitrary symbolism, involving a concatenation of ideas of freedom, the lighthouse, the lighthouse as statue, specifically at Rhodes. Cf. Ch. 3.

16. Gschaedler, op. cit., 13.

17. ibid., 15.

18. Bartholdi, op. cit., 37. For *Liberty*'s lighting, see ch. 7, n. 17.

19. It also might have been connected with Ismail's project for a monument to Mohamed Aly, the cornerstone of which he planned to lay during the Suez ceremonies (Douen, op. cit., II, 431 ff.).

20. Cf. Chapter 1. Gschaedler, op. cit., 14, 20.

21. See Chapter 5.

22. On Scheffer's politics, Egbert, op. cit., 168 ff. His circle included names that reappear among the backers of *Liberty*, e.g., Lafayette, de Lasteyrie.

23. The 'Tombeau des gardes nationaux de Colmar morts en combattant pour la patrie en 1870', or 'Monument Voulminot', 1872 (Salon of 1898, N. 3128); a color illustration is found in Handlin, op. cit., 21. On Bartholdi's attachment to liberty, Mirolli, op. cit., 16; P. DeVèze, 'L'Oeuvre de Bartholdi et l'idée de liberté', *Saisons d'Alsace*, XXIII (1954), 189 ff. (overstated).

24. Gschaedler, op. cit., 6 f.

25. ibid., 51 ff.

26. ibid., 79. Curiously, the face of a large *Liberty* version in the Musée Bartholdi faintly resembles not Bartholdi's

mother but the portrait of his wife in the museum – evidently a transient notion. Another example of such projection of loved ones into contemporary allegorical and historical representation is Thomas Couture's most successful work, *Romans of the Decadence* (1847), from the center of which his future wife gazes out 'wearily' (Boime, op. cit. [1969], 54). In this context it is interesting to note that there appears to be a crypto-signature of Bartholdi on his colossus in the depths of the folds of the lower front cascade, visible from a front-right oblique viewpoint, in the form of a raised 'B' (a frequent monogram on his sketches [16]) [118].

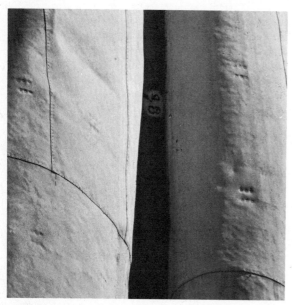

118. Statue exterior showing raised B in fold

3. LIBERTY *(pages 63-83)*

1. Pauly-Wissowa, *Realencyclopädie* (Stuttgart, 1926), XIII, 101 ff.; cf. H. Mattingly, *Roman Coins from the Earliest Times to the Fall of the Western Empire* (London, 1962), 66 f.

2. J. Renouvier, *Histoire de l'art pendant la révolution considéré principalement dans les estampes* (Paris, 1863), 394 ff., stresses the bonnet as the key attribute and gives a history of its continuous employment, including during the Middle Ages (as a sign at commencement of graduating Ph.D.'s and artisans).

3. Ripa's *Iconologia* first appeared in 1593, with an illustrated edition following in Rome, 1603. I use the ample edition of Perugia, 1766, ed. C. Orlandi.

4. See E. Mâle, 'La clef des allégories peintes et sculptées au XVIIe et au XVIIIe siècle', *Revue des deux mondes*, XXXIX (1927), 375 ff., on the development of canonical iconography in general and the continuing importance of Ripa (and imitators) into the nineteenth century (Ripa's last printing was 1764). On liberty, 391 ff. Cf. Renouvier, op. cit., 400 ff.

5. Mâle, op. cit. (mentioning Augustin Dupré's 1776 medal celebrating American *Liberté* [along standard Ripaesque lines]); Renouvier, op. cit., 400 ff. (with a wealth of examples); J. A. Leith, *The Idea of Art as Propaganda in France, 1750–1799* (Toronto, 1965), 106, 108, 120, 122 f. Cf. Lequeu's *Parisis Gate* (or *Arch of the People*) project that saved him from the guillotine in 1793 (*Visionary Architects*, ed. D. de Ménil [Houston, 1968], Fig. 120).

6. Gathered conveniently in M. Reed, *Cowles' Complete Encyclopedia of U.S. Coins* (New York, 1969).

7. L. Taft, *The History of American Sculpture* (New York, 1924), 72 ff., fig. 8 (the bizarre statue is 19 feet tall). Cf. the anticipation of Bartholdi's statue that appeared in a *New York Tribune* editorial of 1875 (from Richard Butler *Liberty* papers, N.Y. Public Library). 'In view of the climate, it may be presumed that Liberty will be draped. Indeed, she is always represented as wearing a sort of disheveled nightdress . . . There are those who believe the Genius of American Liberty should be clad in trousers. No Frenchman, however, can be found who shares this delusion, and if the artist will only spare us the odious Phrygian cap, we shall be entirely contented with the orthodox style of drapery . . .'

8. Cf. Mâle, op. cit., 392 ff.; Sloane, op. cit., 38 n. 8; E. H. Gombrich, 'Icones Symbolicae: Philosophies of Symbolism and their Bearing on Art', *Symbolic Images* (London, 1972), 123 ff.

9. Novotny, op. cit., 220 ff.; Mirolli, op. cit., 17 ff. On the Baroque-Neo-Classical alternatives, J. Selz, *Modern Sculpture*, tr. A. Michelson (New York, 1963), 80 f.

10. E. Panofsky, *Studies in Iconology* (New York, 1967), 70 f.

11. Cf. Boime's illuminating discussion of this process, operative in the 1848 competition for a figure of the Republic (op. cit. [1971]) with explicit mention of *Liberty* (n. 55); also the remarks of Licht, op. cit., 33.

12. Illustrated in A. Dayot, *La révolution française* (Paris, 1896), 100.

13. M.-L. Biver, *Le Paris de Napoléon* (Paris, 1963), 199 ff. In one project (fig. 50) the elephant's burden is inscribed 'Liberté'.

14. 1831–40; 50.33 meters (including the 4 meter sculpture); architecture by Alavione and Duc; the gilded bronze figure the *chef d'oeuvre* of A.-A. Dumont (Hautecoeur, op. cit., VI, 51 ff.; J. Stirling, *Histoire et description de la Colonne de Juillet* [La Cité, 1914]). Dumont was another of those academics whose careers – a predictable sequence of Salon medals, Institut and Légion d'Honneur memberships, École professorships – provided a model for Bartholdi (cf. Chapter 2, n. 11). A bronze copy of the Genius of Liberty was ordered for the Louvre in 1885 by the administration of Beaux-Arts.

15. Although G. H. Hamilton argues strongly that Delacroix probably did not have Barbier's poem in mind ('The Iconographical Origins of Delacroix's "Liberty Leading the People"', *Studies in Art and Literature for Belle da Costa Greene* [Princeton, 1954], 55 ff.) the traditional association, going back to the mid-nineteenth century, retains at least the ring of poetic truth.

16. ibid., 66.

17. Scheffer not only took part in the events of July 1830, but commemorated them in a painting (Egbert, op. cit., 170).

18. On Delacroix's *Liberty*, ibid., 170 ff.

19. Given at the Opera benefit (Gschaedler, op. cit., 39).

20. Boime (op. cit. [1971], 76) stresses the shift from the violence of Rude and Delacroix to a more temperate style of expression in public imagery at mid-century.

21. According to Boime (op. cit. [1969], 54), the Delacroix was 'the last 19th century work in which actuality and personification of abstract qualities or virtues are viably mixed'.

22. J. Selz, op. cit., 80 f., captures this flavor well, also M. Rheims, op. cit., 225 ff.

23. It is conceivable that the appearance of the nimbus in Bartholdi's project was connected as well with a rare medieval depiction of Liberty (and not the usual *Liberalitas*) at Chartres Cathedral, in the Virtue series of the voussoirs of the left portal, north transept, where she assumes the guise of her scholastic sisters (whom she leads) and is crowned by a large nimbus disc (and originally held up another attribute in her damaged right arm). The comparatively insignificant carving would have been known to Bartholdi through its prominent place in Didron's popular handbook (A. N. Didron, *Iconographie chrétienne* (Paris, 1843), 86) where the sculptor could have stumbled upon its illustration in pursuing the lead section of the book, on the nature and use of the nimbus. This

example of the pre-eminent medieval monument, although insufficient to have motivated Bartholdi's notion, could have at least justified his iconographic innovation. (The Chartres example is mentioned also by Renouvier, op. cit., 400 f.).

24. Martin van Heemskerck's 'colossus Solis' of 1572 omits the crown, but Fischer von Erlach returns it to Helios in his famous *Historische Architektur* (1721), including as evidence for his restoration several ancient coins of Helios. Cf. G. Kunoth, *Die historische Architektur Fischers von Erlach* (Dusseldorf, 1956), 43 f.

25. C. Mango, *The Art of the Byzantine Empire, 312–1453, Sources and Documents* (New Jersey, 1972), 251 (my thanks to H. W. Janson for this reference).

25A. For Canova's probable source and a general discussion of the figure and its successors, including the *Statue of Liberty* ('una lontana ma evidente derivazione'), see A. Busiri Vici, 'La statua della Religione del Canova e le sue vicende', *Palatino*, X (1966), 228 ff. Although rare, the radiant crown was not unknown between antiquity and Bernini (e.g., Taddeo di Bartolo); cf. J. Seznec, *The Survival of the Pagan Gods*, tr. B. Sessions (New York, 1961).

26. Illustrated in Zeitler, op. cit., figs. 436, 399 f. On the Elias Robert, *et al.*, see ch. 5 and n. 2.

27. Bartholdi could have taken this from Didron, op. cit., 34. Interestingly, a proposal of William Barton (1782) for the reverse of the Great Seal of the United States included 'the Genius of the American Republic', a lady in white wearing 'a radiated Crown of Gold, encircled with an azure Fillet spangled with Silver Stars', signifying that 'no earthly crown shall rule here'; G. Hunt, *The History of the Seal of the United States* (Washington, 1909), 27 ff.

28. Betz, op. cit., 11 ff., 18.

29. By Johannes Benk (1814-1914); cf. A. Lhotzky, *Die Baugeschichte der Museen und der Neuen Burg* (Vienna, 1941), 87, 173 (my thanks to Professor Dr. R. Wagner-Rieger for this reference and the date of the figure, 1876-8).

30. Gschaedler, op. cit., 39. This kind of distinction was important also to Americans. A pamphlet of Charles C. Coffin, *Building the Nation* (New York, 1882), explicitly contrasts American liberty (a seated, allegorical liberty holding the scales of justice and the constitution) with the French (a ferocious female rushing forward over a decapitated corpse carrying a sword and a trident with a head on it). In the New York *World* of 29 October 1886, 4, it is stated that 'The torch of the Great Statue is not illumined by the glare of error but by the blaze of truth; not by a fire to destroy but by a flame

to enlighten . . .'

31. Brought to my attention by Colin Eisler.

32. For Janet-Lange's painting, see Boime, op. cit. (1971), 77, to which it should be added that the painting's title at the Musée Carnavalet is *La France éclairant le monde*. For the Carpeaux see E. Chesneau, *J. B. Carpeaux* (Paris, 1880), 102.

33. Appearing already on the obverse of A. Dupré's famous *Libertas Americana* medal of 1782, the 1776 reference was one of several traditional ways of Americanizing the Goddess of Liberty, according to E. McClung Fleming, 'From Indian Princess to Greek Goddess, The American Image, 1783–1815', *Winterthur Portfolio*, III (1967), 56 ff. Others: *Liberty* holding or dressed in the American flag [cf. 110]; supporting the American shield; guarded by an eagle [110]; associated with thirteen stars. A parallel to *Liberty*'s two handed iconography may be observed in an 1875 project by Falguierre for a quadriga to surmount the Arc de Triomphe de l'Étoile: the central figure holds up a torch in her one hand and in the other bears a tablet inscribed 'Droits' (C. Simond, *Paris de 1800 à 1900* [Paris, 1900], III, 113).

34. The full program of the project foreshadows Bartholdi's, for David's statue, 'imposante par son caractère de force et de simplicité' was to bear on its breast 'Nature, Verité', and on its arms, 'Force, Courage', anticipating Bartholdi's cumbersome iconographic machinery, as did the even more anticipatory figures of *Liberté* and *Égalité* held in one hand, in David's words 'prêtes à parcourir le monde', the whole intended to 'transmettre à nos descendants le premier trophée élevé par le peuple souverain de sa victoire sur les tyrans'. Bartholdi could have known the project through É.-J. Delécluze, *Louis David* (Paris, 1855), 156 f. (cited by del Caso, op. cit., 190 f.).

35. Taft, op. cit., 18 f. Houdon was almost commissioned a *Liberty* for the chamber of the House of Representatives in 1805 (a figure was executed in plaster by an Italian, but destroyed in 1814; W. Craven, *Sculpture in America* [New York, 1968], 58). A Canova pupil (Enrico Causici) executed a massive plaster *Liberty* for the old House of Representatives (now in Statuary Hall), 1824-5 (ibid., 66).

36. M. Cerutti, *Les Jardins de Betz* (Paris, 1792), 40 (cited in A. O. Aldridge, *Franklin and his French Contemporaries* [New York, 1957], 78).

37. I, 20 ('c'était la liberté, qui se levait de l'autre côté de l'Atlantique pour éclairer, pour échauffer, pour féconder l'univers . . .'). Laboulaye, an ardent student of Franklin (and material in discovering the MS of his autobiography) would have known the Cerutti passage cited above, which occurs in the context of a Franklin 'dialogue'.

38. Bartholdi, op. cit., 60 f. 'The *Liberty* is the largest work of its kind that has ever been completed. The famous Colossus of Rhodes . . . was but a miniature in comparison. The other reputedly immense statues are also quite small beside this gigantic copper figure. Thus the *Bavaria* in Munich measures 15 meters; *Arminius*, 28 meters; St *Charles Borromeo*, 22 meters. The Column Vendôme is only 44 meters in height, and "Liberty Enlightening the World" measures 46 meters from the base to the top of the torch.' Evidently for Bartholdi a column and a statue amounted to practically the same thing (he carefully excluded the July Column, 51 meters high; cf. n. 14 above). The publication of the 1875 banquet gives 32 meters as the statue's height (Farre, op. cit., 11). This might be a slightly erroneous measurement for the height to the head (*c.* 34 m.) – but possibly the project in 1875 was smaller than the definitive version. *Liberty*'s famous measurements are: (in meters) height from base to torch, 46.08 (or 151′ 1″); to crown, 35.50; from heel to top of head, 34 (111′); forefinger length, 2.45 (7′ 11″); circumference of forefinger at second joint, 1.44 (4′ 9″); nail, .33 by .26 (13″ by 10″); height of head, 4.40 (13′ 6″); width of eye, .65 (28″); length of nose, 1.12 (3′ 9″); length of largest ray in crown, *c.* 3.50 (11′ 6″). Her weight includes 80,000 kilograms of copper and 120,000 of wrought iron. With her pedestal of 27.12 meters (89′) and foundations of 16.1 meters (52′ 10″), weighing 25,668 metric tons (28,300 tons) and set 3.96 meters (13′) above mean low water, the monument rises a total of 93.26 meters (305′ 11″) above mean low water sea level.

39. Gschaedler, op. cit., illustration facing p. 42.

40. American Committee of the French-American Union, *Inauguration of the Statue of Liberty Enlightening the World by the President of the United States* (New York, 1887), 32.

4. THE COLOSSAL VISION (*pages 84-101*)

1. See Ch. 7, n. 23.

2. On these Napoleonic projects, Biver, op. cit., 155 ff., 187 ff., 199 ff.: cf. Rosenblum, *Transformations*, 132 f. On Dejoux's *Desaix*, cf. H. W. Janson, 'Observations on Nudity in Neo-Classical Art', *Stil und Überlieferung in der Kunst des Abendlandes, Akten des 21. Internationalen Kongresses für Kunstgeschichte in Bonn 1964* (Berlin, 1967), 198 ff. On David's pet project, see ch. 3, n. 34 and especially D. L. Dowd, *Pageant-Master of the Republic, J.-L. David and the*

French Revolution (Lincoln, Nebraska, 1948), 130 ff. David's enthusiasm for the idea was so extreme that the Convention decreed that, in addition to the colossal bronze, the figure should appear on the State Seal and new coins. Conceivably David's *France-as-Hercules*, intended as a symbol of victory over tyranny (the pedestal was to be composed of fragments of smashed royal statuary), was partly inspired by notions of the American Revolution. Both Adams and Franklin suggested Hercules as a U.S. symbol, and it was proposed to the first Congressional Committee (1776). The reverse of the *Libertas Americana* medal of Augustin Dupré ('Graveur-Général des Monnaies de la République') of 1782 depicted America as the infant Hercules strangling two serpents, representing the British armies of Saratoga and Yorktown (McClung Fleming, op. cit., 53 ff.).

3. The *Virgin* of Le Puy is by Bonnasieux; the Marseilles figure was executed by Lequesne, who worked on the decoration of the Palais de Longchamp. On Bartholdi's involvement in Marseilles, Betz, op. cit., 55 ff. Interestingly, Espérandieu was a student of Vaudoyer, a member of the group around Labrouste that continued the visionary tradition of the late eighteenth century; a fellow student, Lisch, was responsible for one of the 1852 lighthouse competition projects ([13], 2nd from left). *Notre-Dame de France* of Le Puy has nationalist overtones; it was cast from cannons captured in the Crimean War, and its history involved a competition with more than fifty entries (cf. Lesbazeilles, op. cit., 323). The Marseilles figure was a symbol of the city; the Virgin, being patroness of seamen, blesses the ships at sea. Cf. the smaller colossal Madonna – *Notre-Dame des Dunes* (1872) – overlooking the Clain river at Poitiers, on a high socle with a viewing platform; and the similar *Virgin* blessing the ships sailing from the port at Messina (inscribed: VOS ET IPSAM CIVITATEM BENEDICIMUS).

4. *Les Grands Prix de Rome d'Architecture, 1850–1904*, ed. A. Guérinet (Paris, 1850 ff.), pls. 93 (1867), 159 (1876), 169 (1878), for examples. The Neo-Classic attachment to these works was codified by Quatremère de Quincy in his *Jupiter Olympien* (composed in the closing eighteenth century, published 1814) and is echoed by Bartholdi: 'Phidias executed two colossal statues, in which he succeeded in uniting material grandeur with a true ideal of form . . . masterpieces of chryselephantine sculpture . . . All the ancient authors . . . leave no doubt of the value of these works, and of the profound impression which they produced in the Grecian world' (op. cit., 37 f.).

5. The Colossus of Rhodes, 'qui voyait passer entre ses jambes de petites barques assez mal pontées, ne serait qu'un jouet d'enfant auprès de notre statue' (Farre, op. cit., 37 f.). On the Colossus, H. Maryon, 'The Colossus of Rhodes', *The Journal of Hellenic Studies*, LXXVI (1956), 68 ff., according to which the statue was probably around 120 feet high (slightly more than the traditional height), constructed not of massive cast bronze, but like *Liberty* – in the repoussé technique (Chapter 6 below) on a masonry and iron core; certainly it was not 'astride' the harbor, as Europeans had believed since the Renaissance (except for scholarly minds like Bartholdi [see Chapter 5]).

6. A well-known story, e.g., Vitruvius, II; Plutarch, *Alexander*, 72 (cf. Pauly-Wissowa, op. cit., IV, 2392 f.); see W. Körte, 'Deinocrates und die barocke Phantasie', *Die Antike* XIII (1937), 289 ff.

7. H. W. Janson, 'Giovanni Chellini's "Libro" and Donatello', *Studien zur toskanischen Kunst, Festschrift für Ludwig H. Heydenreich* (Munich, 1964), 131 ff., n. 27. The late medieval *Rolands* discussed by Lesbazeilles (op. cit., 97 f.), such as Halberstadt and Halle, also fall into this category.

8. Bartholdi, op. cit., 38 f.

9. Janson, op. cit.; idem, 'The meaning of the giganti', *Il Duomo di Milano, Congresso Internazionale, Atti (Monografia di Arte Lombarda, I monumenti, III)*, ed. M. L. Gatti Perer (Milan, 1969), 71 ff.; C. Seymour, Jr., *Michelangelo's David* (Pittsburgh, 1967), 21 ff.

10. See n. 7 above. Seymour (op. cit., 34) notes that 'It appears that there was in Florence in the first half of the fifteenth century nothing less than a mystique of the colossus, largely derived by humanistic admiration of the antique', which it seems affected even Alberti. But it was in the sixteenth century that the aspiration was put into general practice; cf. V. Mockler, *Colossal Sculpture of the Cinquecento from Michelangelo to Giovanni Bologna* (Ph.D. Diss., Columbia Univ., 1967), with a count of at least 50 colossal statues or groups of colossi produced in Italy 1500–1600 (xxii).

11. ibid., 5 ff., citing also Francesco Doni's enthusiastic phrase, 'spettacoli veramente sopra tutte l'altre opere umane meravigliosi'.

12. F. Medoni, *Memorie storiche di Arona* (Novarra, 1844), 154 ff. The project was initiated in 1610–14, and completed only in 1696; the design was given by G. B. Crespi of Novarra. Bartholdi's comment, op. cit., 39.

13. According to Benvenuto Cellini and Pomponius Gau-

ricus, full-scale colossi run about three times life size (Mockler, op. cit., xiv).

14. For the Carrara story, G. Vasari, *Le Vite de' più eccellenti architetti, pittori, e scultori italiani*, ed. G. Milanesi (Florence, 1881), VII, 163; Condivi, *Vita di Michelangelo*, Ch. XXIV; Körte, op. cit., 295 ff. For the letter, E. H. Ramsden, *The Letters of Michelangelo* (Stanford, 1963), No. 176; K. Frey, *Die Briefe des Michelagniolo Buonarroti*, ed. H.-W. Frey (Berlin, 1961), 249; idem, *Sammlung ausgewählter Briefe an Michelagniolo Buonarroti* (Berlin, 1899), 260 ff. Interestingly, in both cases the super-colossal is folly for Michelangelo – in one instance the Pope's, in the other Michelangelo's own *dementia* from the deprivations of his months of toil at Carrara for the Julius tomb.

15. V. Malamani, *Canova* (Milan, n.d.), 181 f., 186, 220; E. Bassi, *La Gipsoteca di Possagno di Antonio Canova* (Venice, 1957), 219 ff.; cf. also, A. Quatremère de Quincy, *Canova* (Paris, 1824) and A. Busuri Vici, op. cit. A half-scale copy (i.e., the size of the model, 4.10 meters) was set up in SS. Luca e Martina in Rome. This type of *Faith* seems to have been a particular favorite in Venice: e.g., Giusto Le Court, figure surmounting the attic of the Redentore (seventeenth century); Titian, *Doge Antonio Grimani adoring Faith and S. Marco in Glory* (in the ducal palace). The nine-meter *Faith* in the Staglieno Cemetery in Genoa was executed by Santo Varni *c.* 1850 as part of an ambitious architectural program of Carlo Barabino and G. A. Resasco (C. V. Meeks, 'Pantheon Paradigm', *Journal of the Society of Architectural Historians*, XIX [1960], 143 f., fig. 16; my thanks to John Hunnisak and Dr Manfred Fischer for this reference).

16. J. Physick, *Designs for English Sculpture, 1680–1860* (London, 1969), 41 f.; M. Campbell, 'An Alternative Design for a Commemorative Monument by John Flaxman', *Record of the Art Museum, Princeton University*, XVII (1958), 65 ff. (citing Flaxman's Letter to the *Committee for Raising the Naval Pillar or Monument* [London, 1799], quoted here, and discussing another Britannia project related to a Triumphal Arch design by Boullée). In addition to the drawing in our illustration 42, Flaxman's design was engraved by William Blake for publication, and a model of it is preserved in the Soane Museum. The possible link with David's project was suggested to me by H. W. Janson.

17. For these monuments, Physick, op. cit., *passim*; and also idem, *The Wellington Monument* (London, 1970) in which the curious history of the Wyatts' equestrian *Wellington* unfolds. This unpopular work was mocked relentlessly by *Punch*

during its execution, and after its 'trial' erection in 1846 the Queen decided to remove it, but was dissuaded by the Duke of Wellington himself. It remained *in situ* long after his death in 1852, until 1883 when Hyde Park Corner was redesigned, necessitating moving Burton's arch that had served as the pedestal. The statue down, a new site in London could not be found for such a 'colossus' and it was decided to destroy it. But [Wellington's] army saved it, cut it apart in 1884 and moved it laboriously in 1885 to a small hill at Aldershot, on military scrubland, where it still stands – strangely enough, exiled from London during exactly the same years that *Liberty* was 'exiled' from Paris, for different but not altogether unrelated reasons.

18. L. Dehio, *Friedrich Wilhelm IV von Preussen: ein Baukünstler der Romantik* (Berlin-Munich, 1961), 84 (my thanks to John Fleming for this reference).

19. F. Otten, *Ludwig Michael Schwanthaler* (Munich, 1970), 60 ff. Schwanthaler's intention was 'für München wieder eine neue Art von Kunstwerken [zu gewinnen] . . . einen Koloss, wie er als Athene . . . auf der Akropolis von Athen das Parthenon überragte' – referring to the *Athena Promachos* after which the *Bavaria* was modelled, with Bavarian iconographic adaptations.

20. H.-E. Mittig, 'Zu Joseph Ernst von Bandels Hermannsdenkmal im Teutoburger Wald', *Lippische Mitteilungen aus Geschichte und Landeskunde*, XXXVII (1968), 200 ff.; M. Kuhn ed., *K. F. Schinkel, Lebenswerk*; L. Schreiner, *Westfalen* (Deutscher Kunstverlag, 1969), 168 ff. (with illustration of the Schinkel projects).

21. Designed by Johannes Schilling (Dresden), dedicated by Kaiser Wilhelm I in 1883, and carrying in the center of a long inscription a reference to the chauvinist song, 'Die Wacht am Rhein'.

22. Cf. Mirolli, op. cit., 14 f.

23. E.g., the print of the *Bavaria* in execution by G. Hahn of 1860 (illustration in C. Hohoff, *München* [Munich, 1970], 134–5). My thanks to John Fleming for this reference.

24. See note 3 above.

25. See Chapter 7, n. 17

26. Except for his bizarre, rather than brutalist Soldiers' and Sailors' Monument at Indianapolis of 1888–93 (illustration D. Tselos, 'Richardson's Influence on European Architecture', *Journal of the Society of Architectural Historians*, XXIX [1970], 156 ff., fig. 1) Schmitz's major works are illustrated heavily in Wasmuth, op. cit., figs. 106 ff.; cf. also F. Schumacher, *Strömungen in deutscher Baukunst seit 1800*

(Leipzig, 1935); F. Roh, *Geschichte der deutschen Kunst von 1900 bis zur Gegenwart* (Munich, 1958); and the Thieme-Becker entry.

27. H.-R. Hitchcock, *Architecture: Nineteenth and Twentieth Centuries* (Harmondsworth, 1968), fig. 81.

28. In the arid megalomania of Gutzon Borglum's sixty-foot faces of American presidents on Mt Rushmore (on the scale of men 465 feet tall), 1927–41, might be seen a fore-shadowing of the arrogant superpower of the United States following the Second World War – an American parallel to what Bruno Schmitz presaged for Germany. Russia's *Motherland* (illustration Handlin, op. cit., 167), commemorating the Battle of Stalingrad, dedicated in 1967 as the world's tallest sculpture (a fearsome 270-foot female) is another example of this mode (to say nothing of the monuments of the Third Reich; cf. H. Rosenburg, 'The Academy in Totalitaria', *Art News Annual*, XXXIII [1967], 115 ff.). In contrast to the distressing nature of the German, Russian, and American monuments, the Victor Emmanuel Monument in Rome (C. Meeks, *Italian Architecture 1750-1914* [New Haven, 1966] 189 ff.), although sharing their pretensions, seems rather an overinflated piece of foolishness. The French counterpart of these is not the *Statue of Liberty* or the Sacré Coeur (etc.), but the Grand Prix projects of 1890 for a monument to Jeanne d'Arc, particularly Pontremoli's winning entry (Guérinet, op. cit., fig. 356). Somewhere in this chapter should be mentioned the 37-foot *William Penn* atop the 548 foot Philadelphia City Hall (at the time of its construction, 1869–81, the world's highest building), executed *c.* 1872–80 by Alex Milne Calder (grandfather of Alexander Calder); cf. F. Faust, *The City Hall, Philadelphia, Its Architecture, Sculpture, and History* (Philadelphia, 1897).

5. THE SITE (*pages 103-118*)

1. Boime, op. cit., 1971, figs. 23, 24 (Scheffer); 9 (Gérôme); 6 (Cornu).

2. In the Musée Bartholdi there is a model closely resembling the *Navigation* [36] at the Guichet du Carrousel at the New Louvre (1861–4) by Jouffroy, whose ponderous Neo-Classical manner seems the closest to Bartholdi of all the sculptors working on Napoleon III's large projects: cf. also his *Poetry* alongside Carpeaux's *Dance* at the Opera (C. Garnier, *Le Nouvel Opéra de Paris* [Paris, 1875], vol. I, fig. 2). Such figures were painted by Bartholdi's friend Gérôme (see n. 1 above). As mentioned on p. 74, Robert's *La France*

couronnant *Art et Science* was modelled on his master's *Aux grandes hommes la Patrie reconnaissante* at the Panthéon, which in turn was a more modestly clothed and less fluid version of Cartelier's bare-breasted *Victory distributing crowns* at the Louvre East Façade, 1807. One of Elias Robert's fellow students under David d'Angers was J.-F. Soitoux (1816–92) – briefly Bartholdi's teacher – the high point of whose short career was his *La République*, ordered in 1848 by the state, executed in marble by 1850 (Salon no. 3591) at the cost of 1000 Fr., then stored in the State Depots until 1880 when it was set up before the Palais de l'Institut (C. de Vinck and A. Vuaflart, *La Place de l'Institut, 1660-1880* [Paris, 1928], fig. 218). But apart from its theme, this mediocre figure, with a single-star diadem, a shield and a down-turned sword, had little direct connection with the work of Soitoux's student – unlike several other projects for the 1848 Republic Competition, mentioned above. Cf. ch. 2, n. 1.

3. Lefebvre's painting (on which cf. R. Rosenblum, 'Ingres, Inc.', *Art News Annual*, XXXIII [1967], 75) might be compared with the figure of *Truth* on the Palais de Justice (facing the left bank) and another sculpture of the same subject by Jules Calelier (L. Bénédite, *Les sculpteurs français contemporains* [Paris, 1901], pl. XIV).

4. The first practical electric incandescent light was developed by Edison in 1879; by 1884 electrical jewelry was the vogue in Paris – glass cut to imitate gems, fitted into an envelope surrounding a small lamp (powered by a small battery carried by the person) which, shining through, gave the appearance of precious stones (R. Gilbert, *American Jewelry: From the Gold Rush to the Art Nouveau* [Master's thesis, New York Univ., 1962]).

5. Holliman, op. cit., 53. R. M. Hunt, architect of *Liberty*'s pedestal after 1881, built the great W. K. Vanderbilt N.Y. house in 1878.

6. Betz, op. cit., 29, 37 ff., 42, for contemporary criticism, which, though strongly appreciative of the figure's ambitious energy, notes its awkward aspects. For an appreciation of *Ney*, see H. W. Janson, *History of Art* (New York, 1962).

7. Panofsky, op. cit., 174 f.

8. '. . . l'allure des petits chevaux de carrousel . . .' (Betz, op. cit., 77 f.).

9. Bartholdi, op. cit., 35.

10. Bartholdi tried to sell the arm to Philadelphia, where it was exhibited at the 1876 Centennial, not merely to raise funds, but to improve on it in a second version (Betz, op. cit., 135).

11. Bartholdi, op. cit., 37. The Assyrian antiquities were rediscovered by French and British archaeologists beginning mainly in the 1840s, and great public enthusiasm was generated by the works removed to London and Paris, well published in such tomes as *Monument de Ninive découvert et décrit par M. P. E. Botta, mesuré et dessiné par M. E. Flandin*, 5 vols (Paris, 1849) and V. Place, *Ninive et l'Assyrie, avec des essais de restauration par F. Thomas*, 3 vols (Paris, 1866-9). Cf. H. V. Hilprecht, *Explorations in Bible Lands During the 19th Century* (London, 1903), 73 ff. In connection with *Liberty*'s kinetic properties, one might mention the photographic study of animal bodies in motion, developing from the 1850s and culminating in Muybridge's *Animal Locomotion* of 1887 (and eventually motion pictures); the influence of instantaneous photography on avant-garde artists like Manet and Degas; Rodin's interest in 'the progressive development of movement' (F. Popper, *Origins and Development of Kinetic Art*, tr. S. Bann [Greenwich, Conn., 1968], 11 ff.; B. Newhall, *The History of Photography* [New York, 1964], 83 ff.; A. E. Elsen, *Rodin* [New York, 1967], 27 ff.); and of course the visionary leap of the Brooklyn Bridge over Emma Lazarus's 'air-bridged harbor' (cf. A. Trachtenberg, *Brooklyn Bridge* [New York, 1965]). In the 1870s and 1880s fourth-dimensional art was in the air, and even an academic like Bartholdi may have been indirectly affected. James Holderbaum has suggested to me as another parallel to *Liberty*'s double image Poussin's favorite Roman statue, the *S. Susanna* in the Madonna di Loreto by F. Duquesnoy (1629-33). Restoring its original position in the church, one's initial impression would have been a dynamic gesture towards the altar, resolving frontally into a stable *contrapposto*.

12. *Liberty*'s site was claimed for the East India Company in 1609 by Henry Hudson. In 1664, with the British Conquest, it became part of New York, and was acquired by Isaac Bedloe in 1667 (whose name clung to it until 1956, when it was officially renamed Liberty Island, which the public has accepted). From 1732-46, Love Island, as it was officially designated in 1670, was used as a quarantine station during smallpox and other epidemics. 1746-57 saw it as a summer place for Archibald Kennedy, but in 1759 Kennedy Island was bought by New York City as a 'pest House'. In 1776, known as Corporation Island, it was a Tory refuge, and was raided by patriots. A French navy hospital was permitted on the site 1793-6. Finally in 1800 it was acquired by the U.S. government for a fort, and Fort Wood was built 1808-11 on the design of Col. Jonathan Williams. Its last use before being turned over to the *Liberty* project in 1877 was as a Civil War recruitment camp and ordnance depot.

13. Licht, op. cit., 33, stresses Bartholdi's 'technical brilliance' and creativity in integrating monument and site.

6. CONSTRUCTION (*pages 119-150*)

1. Bartholdi, op. cit., 43 ff., for a brief chronological description of the construction. C. Talansier, 'La Statue de la Liberté éclairant le monde', *Le Génie Civil*, III, 1 August 1883, 461 ff., for a detailed technical account of the statue and its structure, including calculations [74-6]. For *Liberty*'s dimensions, see ch. 3, n. 38.

2. Maryon, op. cit., 69 f., on Rhodes. For the structure of the *Athena Parthenos*, G. P. Sevens, in *Hesperia* 24 (1955), 240 ff.; B. Ashmole, *Architect and Sculptor in Classical Greece* (New York, 1972), 97.

3. Bartholdi, op. cit., 39 (underestimating the thickness of *S. Carlo* by a critical half-millimeter). The 9 meter *Hercules* at Kassel is another example of this technique.

4. Hautecoeur, op. cit., VI, 237. Talansier, op. cit., 462 f. Concerning its earlier use in France, Jean Bullant mentions the material in his 1553 edition of Vitruvius, stressing its use for ornamentation (ed. Ferrand, 326; my thanks to Laura Camins for this reference); cf. M. Barbedienne, *Report of the Jury of the Universal Exposition of 1867, class 22*, on hammered work before 1800. One might note the aesthetic confusion of Talansier who notes that repoussé is not only stronger and lighter, but 'Son travail est en outre beaucoup plus originel et plus artistique, puisqu'il se fait entièrement à la main' (op. cit., 463).

5. ibid. The shop, still extant in the early 1960s (when owned by Miège, Buhler & Cie.), was at 25 Rue Chazelles. Bartholdi's own studio was 40 Rue Vavin until 1893, thereafter 82 Rue d'Assas.

6. P.-M. Auzas, *Eugène Viollet-le-Duc* (Paris, 1965), 128. The sculptor preferred stone, but was persuaded. The work was constructed by MM. Monduit et Bechet, the predecessors of MM. Gaget, Gauthier et Cie., responsible for *Liberty* (Talansier, op. cit., 463).

7. ibid., 462, figs. 2f. Bartholdi's statement that the *S. Carlo* was 'the first example of the use of repoussé copper mounted on iron trusses' is doubly erroneous, not only regarding the nature of *S. Carlo* but concerning the lack of earlier examples. According to Maryon (op. cit., 69) the structure of the Colossus of Rhodes combined masonry and ferrous construction supporting the thin repoussé copper skin (Bartholdi, like everyone else, appears to have still believed the Colossus was

a massive casting with a massive masonry interior [op. cit., 38]).

8. A hitherto unknown detail of his career.

9. On his radicalism, Egbert, op. cit., 207 ff. Also Auzas, op. cit., *passim*. Personal contact with Bartholdi might have been arranged by Edmond About, a journalist who had written in praise of the Bartholdi family (particularly Mme B.) after a visit to sundered Alsace in 1871 (Gschaedler, op. cit., 34) and in whose periodical, the *XIXe siècle*, appeared numerous contributions by Viollet-le-Duc in 1874–6 (Auzas, op. cit., 194 ff.). See also Betz, op. cit., 24. His theoretical tract *Entretiens sur l'architecture* (Paris, 1860–72) contained the phrase, 'Intellects of the highest order are produced and matured only by liberty' (*Discourses on Architecture*, tr. B. Bucknell [New York, 1889] II, 436). The *Entretiens* first appeared in fascicules beginning *c.* 1860, collected into the two volumes published in 1863 and 1872 (Hitchcock, op. cit., 455 n. 197). Compare Winckelmann's statement a century earlier: 'Liberty, only liberty has elevated art to perfection' (cited by Honour, op. cit., 69). Albert Boime has brought to my attention a letter addressed to the Emperor in *Le Moniteur Universel*, 29 November 1863, approving the pedagogical reforms enacted by the state on 13 November 1863, in large measure created by Viollet-le-Duc. It was signed by Bartholdi – and by Daubigny, Barye, Huet and Baudot, the pioneer in concrete architecture, among others.

10. Farre, op. cit., 11. 'The words are not Viollet-le-Duc's own, but the editor's description, which is preceded by a characterization of the standard arrangement: 'Les monuments du même genre ont à l'intérieur d'une couche épaisse de maçonnerie, bâtie autour de l'armature en fer, et adhérente à l'enveloppe extérieure.'

11. Cf. n. 9 above.

12. The head was brought to the site on a cart drawn by 12 horses, 28 June 1878 (Betz, op. cit., 143). Bartholdi boasted that 'About forty persons were accommodated in the head at the Universal Exposition of 1878' and that the torch 'will easily hold twelve persons' (op. cit., 52).

13. There is no definitive work on Eiffel. For his biography and career see J. Prevost, *Eiffel* (Paris, 1929); M. Besset, *Gustave Eiffel* (Milan, 1957); R. Barthès and A. Martin, *La Tour Eiffel* (Paris, 1964); S. Giedion, *Space, Time, and Architecture* (Cambridge, Mass., 1967), 238 ff., 263 ff., 277 ff.

14. Cf. F. D. Klingender, *Art and the Industrial Revolution*, ed. A. Elton (London, 1968), 182 ff.

15. (New York, 1891), 30 f.

16. e.g., the Magasin au Bon Marché in Paris, with the architect L. A. Boileau (Giedion, op. cit. [1967], 52 ff.); railroad stations at Toulouse, Agen, St Sebastien, Santander, Lisbon, and especially Pesth; the Nice observatory, with Charles Garnier (Prevost, op. cit., 52 ff.). For a catalogue of works, 1867–90, see the appendix in Eiffel's magnificent two-volume folio (one of the most beautiful books of the century), *La Tour de Trois Cents Mètres* (Paris, 1900). Eiffel was innocently involved in the Panama Canal scandal of 1893, and eventually was absolved of blame. Late in life he was preoccupied with aerodynamics, a concern all along (especially in the high bridges), and established certain aerodynamic laws around 1909–12.

17. G. Eiffel, *Notice sur le Viaduc du Garabit* (Paris, 1888).

18. Cf. Giedion, op. cit. (1967), 279 ff.; Prevost, op. cit., 13 ff., 25 ff.

19. The great theme of Giedion, op. cit. (1967).

20. G. Tissandier, *La Tour Eiffel de 300 mètres* (Paris, 1889).

21. G. Eiffel, 'The Eiffel Tower', *Smithsonian Institution Annual Report*, July 1889, 735. Cf. G. Tissandier, *The Eiffel Tower* (London, 1889), 'In front of the Champ de Mars, the Eiffel Tower rising from its four iron piers forms the arch of the triumph of science and industry'; *Conference de M. Eiffel sur la Tour de 300 mètres* (Paris, 1889), '. . . elle forme une entrée triomphale de l'Exposition'. Speaking for the engineering profession, L. F. Vernon-Harcourt, *Achievements in Engineering during the Last Half-century* (New York, 1892), 301, writes that Eiffel's bridges 'unite the boldness of the tower with far greater simplicity and a distinctly greater elegance' and that 'the renown of the tower is due to its absolutely unrivaled height, the occasion of its erection, and its position in the most popular capital of the world, but it is unquestionable that the Garabit Viaduct, the Antwerp quays, the Danube and Mississippi delta works . . . the Severn tunnel, the Brooklyn and Forth bridges . . . are far greater engineering triumphs.'

22. Cf. R. Banham, *Theory and Design in the First Machine Age* (London, 1960).

23. Giedion, op. cit. (1967), 281.

24. Cf. ibid. and especially Eiffel's own publications.

25. G. Mehrtens, *A Hundred Years of German Bridge Building* (Berlin, 1900), fig. 103. Cf. also the bridge over the Aar near Berne, 1898, B. H. Fischer architect (W. J. Watson, *Bridge Architecture* [New York, 1927], 159). A more understanding derivation of the Garabit is L. L. Buck's Clifton

Bridge at Niagara Falls, 1898 (ibid., 162).

26. Vernon-Harcourt, op. cit., Ch. VI.

27. A. Trachtenberg, op. cit.

28. Eiffel was born in Dijon and, whether he knew it or not, was the heir to the extraordinary technical daring and visual elegance of his Burgundian Gothic ancestors of the twelfth and thirteenth centuries, who built the choirs of Notre-Dame in Auxerre and Dijon, works that were prominently resurrected by Viollet-le-Duc himself, who grew enthusiastic about their structural brilliance. See *Dictionnaire raisonné de l'architecture française du XIe au XIVe siècle* (Paris, 1854-68), IV, 131 ff. So airily spun-out is the metal in the tower that it has been calculated that all the metal reduced to a square the size of the base (125 m.) would be only 6 cm. high; its weight is approximately the same as a cylinder of air of its height and circumscribing its feet; a scale model one foot high would weigh one-fourth of an ounce.

29. Cf. H. Straub, *A History of Civil Engineering*, tr. E. Rockwell (London, 1952), excellent, except for a curious slighting of Eiffel.

30. Talansier, op. cit.; for large photographs of the armature, Gontrand, Reinhard, et compagnie, *Album des travaux de construction de la statue colossale de la Liberté* (Paris, 1888), New York Public Library. For an up-to-date description, C. Condit, *American Building Art - The Nineteenth Century* (New York, 1960), 46, 287 n. 16.

31. Talansier describes what was evidently the tentative means of attachment in Paris: '. . . pour que chaque métal puisse se dilater librement, les armatures en fer, au lieu d'être rivées sur la statue, sont simplement maintenues dans des gaines en cuivre rivées elles-mêmes sur l'enveloppe' (op. cit., 464). Eiffel also provided electric insulation of shellac-impregnated asbestos between iron and copper to prevent galvanic action, and the statue is grounded against lightning (ibid.; Holliman, op. cit., 78 f.).

32. Giedion, op. cit. (1967), 266 ff. Another daring invention of Eiffel in this category was the flotation of the 45 meter diameter Cupola of the Grand Equatorial of the Nice Observatory on an annular mercury ring (1884).

33. Cf. Condit, op. cit., 39 ff., 46.

34. Compare Bartholdi's account ('I can say that at the view of the harbor of New York the definite plan was clear to my eyes,' op. cit., 18) with his letters home in 1871 (Betz, op. cit., 101 ff.). There were objections to Bartholdi's choice (Holliman, op. cit., 5).

35. Condit, op. cit., 229 f., 335 n. 18.

36. Hitchcock, op. cit., 309 ff.; P. Collins, *Concrete, The Vision of a New Architecture* (New York, 1959); A. A. Raafat, *Reinforced Concrete in Architecture* (New York, 1958).

37. Stone was assisted by C. C. Schneider, a civil engineer, in the plan of mounting and pedestal reinforcement. The steel was furnished by the Keystone Bridge Company of Pittsburgh, Pennsylvania (Holliman, op. cit., 51 f.). Condit (op. cit., 46) appears to have confused the use of wrought iron and steel in *Liberty*, also claiming that the armature - shipped with the statue from France - is American.

38. On Art Nouveau, Hitchcock, op. cit., 281.

39. Unlike the torch and right hand, whose original armature of 1876 appears to have been replaced by Eiffel's, it is not certain whether the cage of the head is the original framework of 1878 - probably Viollet-le-Duc's - or is instead a new design like the rest of the armature. Two details would seem to favor the former possibility, however. The massive brackets attaching the shell to the armature differ from the rest of the statue. And the armature itself - in the way the angles are loosely joined to form a T-beam, in the uneven spacing of rivets and holes - manifests a lack of the elegance and precision that seems to characterize everything of Eiffel's (in the Tower, the tolerances were as low as 0.1 mm - even for the rivet holes). The skeletal cage is not shown in Talansier's elaborate publication of Eiffel's calculus and designs (op cit.), which would reinforce the hypothesis that it was not part of Eiffel's contribution. Although it does appear in the cross-section in Besset, op. cit., fig. 4, from Eiffel's shop, this was not a working or calculus rendering but a presentation drawing for the public that included everything regardless of origin. The cross-sections in Fig. 83 are inaccurate regarding the head, and do not include the cage.

40. Hitchcock, op. cit., 281 ff.

41. Museum of Modern Art, *Art Nouveau* (New York, 1967), P. Selz and M. Constantine, ed., 16 (Selz); S. T. Madsen, *Sources of Art Nouveau* (Olso, 1956); R. Schmutzler, *Art Nouveau* (New York, 1962).

42. In 1875 Coney Island was proposed - only half in jest - as a site for *Liberty* as an attraction for pleasure-seekers (*New York Times*, 21 November 1875, 6; Holliman, op. cit., 5).

43. Cf. M. de Nansouty, *La Tour Eiffel* (Paris, 1889), 69: 'Il est beau, intéressant, amusant de monter à une hauteur de 300 metres: ce ne saurait être ne dangereux ne effrayant, surtout quand le voyage se fera, non pas dans la nacelle d'un ballon, main dans d'excellent ascenseurs où la science de nos

ingénieurs aura trouvé encore une belle occasion de manifester la précision et la sécurité de ses etudes.' W. A. Eddy, 'The Eiffel Tower', *The Atlantic Monthly*, LXIII (June, 1889), 723, writes, 'It will take the place of the great balloon let up into the air by means of a cable worked by steam, which was so successful during the Exposition . . . without the danger of collapse or gas explosion caused by lightning . . . the view of Paris at night, with its seemingly interminable boulevards brilliantly lighted, is marvellous, and such as astronauts only have witnessed. The feeling of distance and height will not be lessened by intervening lower slopes as in most mountain views.'

44. ibid.; F. I. Jenkins, 'Harbingers of Eiffel's Tower', *Journal of the Society of Architectural Historians*, XVI, 4 (December 1957), 22 ff.; D. Tselos, op. cit., 156 n. 1; Barthes and Martin, op. cit., 12; Eiffel, op. cit. (Smithsonian), 729 ff.; R. A. Fischer, *Background on the Eiffel Tower* (MS in Avery Memorial Library, Columbia University, 1964). The drive to visionary height did not end with Eiffel. An 1120 foot tower along Eiffel's lines was proposed by George S. Morison for the Columbian Exposition of 1893 (*Engineering News*, 5 December 1891), and in 1890 the Bostonian Edward S. Shaw designed a 1400 foot structure for London's Wembley Park (*Engineering Building Record*, 23 August 1890, 183; Eiffel, op. cit. [1900], fig. 239 along with other projects for the site), a height almost realized in the World Trade Center. Cf. Fischer, op. cit.

45. Eiffel, op. cit. (Smithsonian), 734; cf. his statement at a banquet given the press on the first platform of the Tower on 4 July 1888 (de Nansouty, op. cit., 100 ff.).

46. On the history of the project, the publications of Eiffel himself (cited above) are still the best; cf. Fischer, op. cit.; de Nansouty, op. cit.; Prevost, op. cit. The question of authorship of the project – Eiffel or his talented assistant Koechlin (suggested by Straub, op. cit., 184, and, more tentatively, by Fischer, op. cit., 10 f.) – was confronted by Eiffel himself, who dedicates his great folio volumes to his collaborators, lists the personnel behind the title page, generously thanks Nougier (a major assistant of calculation since the Duoro Bridge) and especially Koechlin for diligent and inspired assistance, but, to put the records straight, concludes, 'I myself directed the definitive studies and the execution with my engineers' (op. cit. [1900], I, 4). In his Smithsonian report he writes, 'The result of these studies [with my staff] led me . . . to propose the erection of the tower, now completed, of which the first plan had been drawn out by two of my chief

engineers, Messrs. Nouguier and Koechlin [Fig. 73]. The fundamental idea of these pylons or great archways is based on a method of construction peculiar to me, of which the principle consists of giving to the edges of the pyramid a curve of such a nature that the pyramid shall be capable of resisting the force of the wind, without necessitating the junction of the edges by diagonals, as is usually done.' The ambition and spirit – the genius – of the monument are in any case Eiffel's, whose three decades of previous development it obviously climaxes, and without whose entrepreneurial talents it would never have been achieved.

47. Prevost, op. cit., 40 f. (*Le Temps*, February).

48. Giedion, op. cit. (1967), 284 f.

49. Eiffel, op. cit. (Smithsonian), 732 f.

50. Eddy, op. cit., 726 f., sets together the Tower, the *Statue of Liberty* (not beautiful, but 'wonderful'), the Brooklyn Bridge, and T. A. Edison's 'Power of thought over the refractory powers of the earth' extending into 'new dimensions'.

7. THE PEDESTAL (*pages 151–178*)

1. Farre, op. cit., frontispiece.

2. A less rusticated, roughly octagonal variation of the project appears in *Scribner's Monthly*, June 1877, 133. In a letter to the editor of the New York *Tribune*, dated 15 October 1875, Laboulaye states that 'the pedestal, with allegories about the history of the United States, will be nearly 75 feet high' and that 'the whole monument from the soil to the summit of the head will attain 200 feet'.

3. A. Quatremère de Quincy, *Dictionnaire historique d'architecture* (Paris, 1832), II, 731.

4. Quatremère de Quincy cautions against the abuse of this possibility (ibid.). Cf. the more positive statement in, for example, E. Lomax and T. Gunyon, *Encyclopedia of Architecture, being a new and improved edition of Nicholson's Dictionary of the Science and Practice of Architecture* (London, 1852), II, 269 (the Anglo-Saxon position, as it were): 'Vignola observes there is no part of architecture more arbitrary, and in which greater liberty may be taken than in the pedestals of statues . . . their form, character, etc., are to be extraordinary and ingenious . . .'

5. Mittig, op. cit., 219 ff.

6. Viollet-le-Duc's great cry was for a new rationalism in architecture; but his rival Garnier noted (fairly) of his actual designs, 'On cherche une personalité, on ne trouve que des compromis. Bridé par l'archéologie, il est écrasé par le poids

du passé . . .' (quoted from *À travers les arts* [Paris, 1869] in Auzas, op. cit., 138). The most famous example of a fortress surmounted by a statue is, of course, the Castel S. Angelo in the Vatican.

6A. On the seal, G. Hunt, op. cit. The official 1782 interpretation (p. 42): 'The pyramid signifies Strength and Duration; the Eye over it and the Motto allude to the signal interpositions of providence in favor of the American cause. The date underneath is that of the Declaration of Independence, and the words under it signify the beginning of the New American Era, which commences from that date.'

7. In Hunt's acceptance speech on receiving the Royal Gold Medal from the R.I.B.A. (*The R.I.B.A. Journal of Proceedings*, IX, n.s. [1893], 425.)

8. At the R.I.B.A. ceremony (see preceding note), where von Guymüller said: 'this distinction falls on an artist of whom old Vasari would no doubt have written: "Fu il primo che introdusse in America il buon disegno". By doing this Mr Hunt has become the Brunellesco of the U.S.'

9. There exists no extensive, let alone definitive work on Hunt. Cf. M. Schuyler, 'The Works of the Late Richard M. Hunt', *Architectural Record*, V (1895), 97 ff.; B. Ferree, 'R. M. Hunt: His Art and Work', *Architecture and Building*, 7 December 1895, 271 ff.; M. Brenner, *R. M. Hunt, Architect* (Master's thesis, New York University, 1944); A. Burnham, 'The New York Architecture of R. M. Hunt', *Journal of the Society of Architectural Historians*, XI (May, 1952), 9 f.; Catherine Clinton Howland, *The R. M. Hunt Papers 1828–1895*, ed. A. Burnham (American Architectural Archive, 65 Fairfield Rd., Greenwich, Conn.) (with the interesting statement, 'No more appropriate architect could have been selected to aid Mons. Bartholdi, for Richard's respect and admiration for *Mons. Laboulaye* [italics mine] was unlimited' [187 f.]). Hunt's works include the Lenox Library (1869–70), the Tribune Building (1873), the W. K. Vanderbilt House (1878 ff.), the 'Breakers' at Newport (1892–5), the Biltmore estate at Ashville, N.C. (1890 ff.), the Fogg Museum (1894–5), the Administration Building of the Columbian Exposition (1893), and the center part of the Fifth Avenue façade of the Metropolitan Museum (with his son Richard Howland Hunt, built 1900–1902). There are also numerous monuments (Howland, op. cit., lists twenty-five), some quite ambitious, e.g., the Yorktown Monument (1881–4), the Wadsworth Monument at Genesco, N.Y. (1887). The building closest in spirit to the symbolic eclecticism of Hunt's *Liberty* pedestal is his Islamesque edifice for the Scroll and Key secret society of Yale College (1867).

10. Betz, op. cit., 154.

11. Hunt's papers and drawings are in the A.I.A. Archive in Washington, D.C. Although the originals were unavailable during my research because of rebuilding, fortunately photographs of the drawings for the *Liberty* pedestal were available at the National Park Service offices.

12. One of the drawings (also inscribed 'monument messicain') is a precise copy, reversed, of the illustration of a Pre-Columbian pyramid (Guatusco) on p. 561 of L. Batissier, *Histoire de l'art monumental* (Paris, 1846). This French source, the French inscription on the drawing, and the note 'in Bartholdi letter July 26/82' – all found also on illustration 89 and partly on illustration 88 – as well as the sketchy character of the draftsmanship are evidence that these are probably Bartholdi's rough indications to Hunt of his various notions (at the moment). Cf. the appearance of the Maya temple in H. Monroe, *John Wellborn Root, A Study of His Life and Work* (Chicago, 1966), facing 250 (my thanks to Eleanor Pearson for this reference).

13. E.g., De Ménil, op. cit., 108.

14. Ferree, op. cit., 271 ff., stresses the scholarly quality of Hunt. Cf. Schuyler, op. cit.

15. S. Serlio, *De architectura libri quinque* (Venice, 1569), 250; Quatremère de Quincy, *Dictionnaire*, 'Bossage'; Viollet-le-Duc, *Dictionnaire*, 'Bossage'; E. Bosc, *Dictionnaire raisonné d'architecture* (Paris, 1883), 'Bossage', whose fig. 10 ('Bossages à carreaux et boutisses') is the most comparable of the Franco-Italian sources to Hunt's drawings. The Sangallo fortress is mentioned in Quatremère de Quincy and in Bosc (and also in J. Burckhardt, *Geschichte der Renaissance in Italien* [Stuttgart, 1878], 205 f.), but achieved real prominence only in G. Clausse, *Les San Gallo* (Paris, 1901), II, 299 ff., whose illustrations, however, flatten out the rustication of the rectangular blocks into ashlar, falsely emphasizing the pattern of the hemispherical bosses; Hunt's sensibility may have been similar. Cf. the photograph in A. Venturi, *Storia dell'arte italiana* [Milan, 1938], XI, I, Fig. 573. (My thanks to Eleanor Pearson for this reference.)

16. Both Plateresque examples were published at the time: e.g., M. Digby Wyatt, *An Architect's Note-Book in Spain* (London, 1872), Pls. 14–19, 78 (with a statement about the Guadalajara palace: 'One might have fancied that every true Spaniard would have regarded this palace almost as a holy place' [181]). Hispanic architecture was not without influence on the architecture of the period; cf. Richardson's use of

Salamanca cathedral (H.-R. Hitchcock, *The Architecture of H. H. Richardson and His Times* [Cambridge–London, 1966], 139 f.).

17. *Liberty* was a carry-over from the Suez project and was intended from the beginning to serve as a lighthouse (one way of justifying it to its supporters). As such it appears in the promotional announcement of the project in 1875: 'At night a luminous aureole projected from the head will radiate on the far flowing waves of the ocean' (Gschaedler, op. cit., facing p. 42). At the Hôtel du Louvre banquet in November a letter is read from Nathan Appleton, Esq. (London) offering 'to furnish free of all expense the necessary light with my burners which are employed in nearly every lighthouse in France and the other countries, to establish this as one of the first and best lights in the world' (*Galignani's Messenger*, 10 November 1875; Hughes, op. cit., 24). The Gounod hymn of 1876 expresses the dualism of symbolism and functionalism (see p. 82 above), which appears in 1877 in the Congressional Resolution of 22 February, accepting the gift and authorizing 'regulations to be made for its permanent maintenance as a beacon, and for the permanent care and preservation thereof as a monument of art . . .' (*Congressional Record*, 44th Congress, 2nd Sess., [H.R. no. 196] p. 1824; cited by Holliman, op. cit., 8 f.).

The lighting of the statue, however, proved to be problematic, not only financially but especially practically (because of the limitations of early electrical engineering). As late as 1883 it was still intended to restrict the light to the diadem; the torch was 'reserved for lookouts' (Talansier, op. cit., 466). By 1885, in addition to the radiance of the diadem windows, it was planned to electrify the torch, the thought being to send up a great vertical beam that would be seen far at sea, especially when illuminating passing clouds (proposed by General Stone [New York *World*, 22 April 1885, 5]). In 1886 two rows of circular holes were cut in the torch for this purpose, but the projection was disappointing (like a 'glow worm'), hardly visible even from the harbor. Arc lamps of considerable power were set up on the ground to illuminate the statue itself, but they also proved inadequate, particularly as the statue darkened. In 1887 Bartholdi was asked for advice, which was that the statue could be properly illuminated provided it were covered with gold or some other shining metal. A brief experiment with color followed in 1892: red and yellow light from the torch, red, white and blue from the diadem (recalling the century's preoccupation with polychromy since Quatremère de Quincy). When Bartholdi visited the statue the next

year, he was still disappointed with the lighting, and again suggested gilding. (Richard Butler, *Liberty* papers, N.Y. Public Library, MSS Division: Bartholdi to D. P. Heap 7 September 1893).

In the following years things went from bad to worse before improving, lighting even being suspended for periods from lack of funds. The turning point in the fate of *Liberty*'s lighting came in 1902, when it was tacitly recognized that she was not really a lighthouse and was therefore passed from control of the Lighthouse Board (which really had no use for her, and had only inherited her in 1887 because there was no one else) to the War Department (which had originally controlled the fortified island). From this time on the pure symbolic value of the statue was the criterion for illumination. But it was only the Great War that rekindled interest in the symbolism – this time, however, intensely and permanently. A 'loving flame' was now envisioned, and total, brilliant illumination. The War Department, the New York *World* (which thirty years earlier had campaigned successfully for the pedestal fund; see Chapter 8), and U.S. officialdom drummed up the funds; a General Electric lighting expert provided improved technology for the new flood-lighting and projection; and Gutzon Borglum (later of Mt Rushmore) refashioned the torch by cutting away openings over the entire surface (leaving only quite narrow strips of copper so that it might be three-dimensionally luminous, yielding a realistic blaze through 600 square feet of amber glass, powered by a strong lighthouse source (20,000 candlepower) together with a series of flasher lamps to give the varying flicker of a flame.

The emotions aroused by war were responsible for *Liberty*'s newly luminous state, fittingly achieved under the War Department's administration. Her final change in status came at a time of peace two decades later – after further improvements in intensity and evenness of lighting in 1931 – when *Liberty* passed to the office of National Parks of the Department of the Interior (along with similar monuments), her status as a monument finally recognized fully, and her military and lighthouse associations dissolved. Thus given brilliant luminosity as a normal, peacetime condition, the only way to make a statement with *Liberty* during the Second World War, was to turn her lights symbolically *out*. (Cf. Holliman, op. cit., 62 ff., 86 ff. for a full, documented account of the lighting changes and the statue's changing official status.)

18. Most probably windows, according to a personal communication of Bluma Trell. Cf. H. Thiersch, *Pharos, Antike Islam und Occident* (Leipzig and Berlin, 1909).

19. op. cit., (*Dictionnaire*) II, 226. Cf. Thiersch, op. cit.

20. Illustrating Bannister Fletcher's classic textbook of architectural history. Cf. Erasmus Field's *Historical Monuments of the American Republic* (1876), Springfield Museum, Springfield, Mass. (illustration D. M. Mendelowitz, *A History of American Art* [New York, 1964], 417).

21. As late as 27 June 1883, no decision had been made on the two 'Pharos' alternatives (New York *World*, 5); in August, Talansier published the 'Pharos' variant as his frontispiece (op. cit., fig. 1), although Hunt only produced the definitive drawing of the first 'Pharos' project on 16 August 1883; the definitive drawing of the variant is dated 28 May 1884, at a time when it was already being considered to reduce the pedestal height (which occurs definitively in late July/August of 1884). In a letter of 1 February 1884, Bartholdi expresses a preference for Hunt's initial project and hopes that in the changes its 'general character' will be preserved (Betz, op. cit., 160) – probably referring to the 'Pharos' type in contrast to the definitive mode.

22. Bartholdi uses the phrase 'forme parlante' in connection with the project for the Lion of Belfort (Betz, op. cit., 111).

23. E. Kaufmann, *Architecture in the Age of Reason* (Cambridge, Mass., 1955); idem, *Three Revolutionary Architects, Boullée, Ledoux, Lequeu* (Philadelphia, 1952); Hitchcock, op. cit. (1968), xxiv ff., *passim*; de Ménil, op. cit.

24. Compare Hunt's Doric details, embattled cresting, swollen density of forms, and general Ledolcian air with contemporary Grand Prix projects for monuments (many of which, incidentally, include figures with torch and antique crown): Necropolis, 1883, by Redon (Guérinet, op. cit., figs. 269 ff.); to Jeanne d'Arc, 1893, by Pontremoli (ibid., fig. 356); Château d'Eau, 1873, by Ratouin (ibid., fig. 131); Un palais pour l'exposition des Beaux-Arts, 1867, by Emile Bénard (ibid., fig. 90). From Hunt's (and Bartholdi's) student days, Un édifice consacré à la sepulture d'un souverain, by Bonnet (first prize), Vaudremer (second prize) (ibid., figs. 16 ff.). Concerning the forty shields of Hunt's pedestal, *Scientific American*, 13 June 1885, 375.

On the *neo-Grec* triglyph-piers of Hunt's loggia, cf. W. Ames, 'The Transformation of Château-sur-Mer', *Journal of the Society of Architectural Historians*, XXIX (1970), 301 n. 26, for another prominent example in Hunt's work (the *porte cochère* piers, 1872, fig. 16), noting that the form seems to come straight from Michelangelo's tapered pilaster fluting. On the Arthur F. Mathews design see Harvey J. Jones,

Mathews, Masterpieces of the California Decorative Style, The Oakland Museum (Oakland 1972). I am obliged to the editors for this reference.

25. Cf. Schuyler's estimation (op. cit., 114 ff.).

26. On Richardson, Hitchcock, op. cit. (1966); compared with Hunt, 180, *passim*.

27. ibid., 115 (with a high estimate of the resulting effect). Bartholdi may have been introduced to both Richardson and Hunt by his friend John LaFarge, who was a collaborator with Richardson (Trinity Church; ibid., 139 ff.) and a friend of Hunt (until 1887-8 anyway; Howland, op. cit., 43, 111). Levi P. Morton, American Minister to France in the early 1880s, acted as an important intermediary between the French and the American patrons of *Liberty* (Gschaedler, op. cit., 67 ff., 80 f., 97 f., 154), and may have contributed to the choice of Hunt as architect; he had employed him as early as 1869 on his Newport house and again in 1884 for his house in Reinbeck, New York (communication of Nancy Goeschel, supplementing W. Ames, op. cit., 293 n. 10). In the summer of 1885 Hunt visited Paris and snubbed Bartholdi, for unknown reasons, perhaps having to do with the sculptor's preference for his early rather than definitive pedestal designs (Richard Butler *Liberty* papers, New York Public Library, MSS Division: Bartholdi to Butler, 1 February 1884; 4 March 1884; 21 July 1885; 30 July 1885; cf. n. 21 above).

28. Even Hunt's pedestal – whose intended stair platform was never executed – deserved better than to be violated by the U.S. Department of the Interior's architectural staff in its ill-considered Museum of American Immigration, constructed in the early 1960s as two brutal, stepped forms at the foot of the pedestal.

8. THE AMERICANS (*pages 179-196*)

1. The condensed nature of this chapter – which is the major subject (together with Bartholdi biography) of most of the *Liberty* literature – disallows footnoting of sources, with a few exceptions. For a full documented account of the material presented here, Betz, op. cit., 130 ff., 165 ff., 176 ff.; Holliman, op. cit.; Gschaedler, op. cit., 40 ff., 66 ff.

2. T. A. Bailey, op. cit., 427 ff. Just as a number of *Liberty*'s French supporters were Freemasons (Henri Martin the most conspicuous, but also Bartholdi himself [Gschaedler, op. cit., 85; Chapter 1, n. 30 above]), many of Bartholdi's supporters in the U.S. were abolitionists (Sumner being the most famous [the 'Moses of the Black race']). This would appear to sug-

gest – at least for many Americans – that *Liberty* was seen as a monument to the Civil War victory. In 1871 this may have been felt as an undertone, but by the late 1870s the force of the abolitionists was dissipated, Reconstruction abandoned, and American energies turned elsewhere. Neither Freemasonry nor Abolition as such appear consequentially in the sources.

3. Betz, op. cit., 103. Bartholdi naturally regarded this as an obstacle to his ambitions.

4. Witness the mocking of Horatio Greenough's heroic seated, half-nude *Washington* in the 1840s (Craven, op. cit., 108 f.; given the realities of America perhaps the reaction was justified).

5. *New York Times*, 29 September 1876, 4. In 1949 it was proposed to have the shadow of a diplodocus devour her in a revival of Chinese shadow spectacles (Betz, op. cit., 209).

6. 'There seems no hope of a speedy deliverance from this state worship of *Libertas*. She is to remain on our coins, and the gigantic bronze figure will soon tower on the little island in the beautiful bay of New York. Massive and grand, beautiful in outline and in pose, holding her torch to proclaim that mankind receives true light, not from Christ and Christianity, but from heathenism and her gods.' ('Our Great Goddess and her Coming Idol', *American Catholic Quarterly Review*, V [1880], 593.)

7. Gschaedler, op. cit., 134; Holliman, op. cit., 39 f. Much of the criticism appears to have been due to the desire for journalistic sensation (*Liberty* as a disgrace) rather than pure or even personal critical ends. Eastman Johnson was one of the few American artists to praise the statue ('As a colossal work it is magnificent and thoroughly successful'). French criticism was generally approving – even enthusiastic (especially in the context of colossal statuary); cf. Betz, op. cit., 144 ff., 170 f., 197 f.

8. New York *World*, 24 June 1885, 4 (cf. Holliman, op. cit., 5 f.).

9. Cf. Pauli and Ashton, op. cit., ch. IV. Ironically Bartholdi's publicity was overshadowed by the Tilden-Hayes election controversy, not settled until January 1877 when Hayes sold out to the Electoral College to win, in effect abandoning Reconstruction at the very moment when *Liberty*'s fortunes were ascendant.

10. Gschaedler, op. cit., 141.

11. 'Not like the brazen giant of Greek fame,
With conquering limbs astride from land to land;
Here at our sea-washed, sunset gates shall stand

A mighty woman with a torch, whose flame
Is the imprisoned lightning, and her name
Mother of Exiles. From her beacon-hand
Glows world-wide welcome; her mild eyes command
The air-bridged harbor that twin cities frame.
"Keep, ancient lands, your storied pomp!" cries she
With silent lips. "Give me your tired, your poor,
Your huddled masses yearning to breathe free,
The wretched refuse of your teeming shore.
Send these, the homeless, tempest-tost to me,
I lift my lamp beside the golden door!"'

Contrast John Greenleaf Whittier's academic verses that were read at the dedication ceremony to express the official interpretation:

O France, the beautiful! to thee
    Once more a debt of love we owe:
In peace beneath thy fleur-de-lis,
    We hail a later Rochambeau!
Shine far, shine free, a guiding light
    To Reason's ways and Virtue's aim,
A lightning flash the wretch to smite
    Who shields his license with thy name!

Curiously it was the scrupulous critic James Russell Lowell who first recognized the deeper meaning given Liberty by Lazarus (cf. Handlin, op. cit., 57 ff.).

12. Handlin, op. cit., on *Liberty* and the immigrants; also the material in the American Museum of Immigration now at the base of the statue.

13. On American iconography, see New School for Social Research, *Americans in Paris, 1600-1900*, ed. P. Mocsanyi, M. Melot, and others (New York, 1972) and especially E. McClung Fleming, op. cit. In Anglo-American illustration, *Columbia* (counterpart of *Britannia*) was a favorite, and conventionally represented either as a grand, classically-robed female (e.g., *Harper's Weekly*, 3 January 1863; *Puck*, 10 April 1889; Bartholdi's Tiffany trophy [Handlin, op. cit., 63]) or in the guise of the Indian Princess, etc., i.e. in classicizing garments decorated with such specific references as stars (alluding to the flag) or wearing the Indian headdress of *America* (e.g. *Punch*, 6 May 1865; 16 November 1872). Handlin's suggestion (op. cit., 28) of Joel Barlow's figure of Columbia in his famous epic *The Columbiad* (Philadelphia, 1807) as a source for Bartholdi's 'antique robe and upheld torch', appears to be a misreading of the figure of the Visionary Angel, Hesper, who appears to Columbus in prison – and at that, illustrated as a gorgeous *male* with flowing hair and

robes, arms up, and a star-nimbus shining over his head (I, 139; cf. the figure of the *Inquisition* in Book IV facing p. 144, who does have robes and an upheld torch). The epic comes closest to inspiring Bartholdi and Laboulaye at the close of Book I, when Columbus says to the Visionary Angel:

'Unveil . . . my friend, and stretch once more
Beneath my view that heaven-illumined shore;
Let me behold her silver beams expand,
To lead all nations, lighten every land,
Instruct the total race, and teach at last
Their toils to lessen and their chains to cast.'

14. On *Liberty*'s lighting see Chapter 7, n. 17. Two further illustrations of *Liberty*'s turn of meaning appear in G. J. Hecht, *The War in Cartoons* (New York, 1919): 'Die Wacht am Rhein' (p. 189), showing the 'Dough Boy' standing on cliffs over 'The Rhine', cradling a gun in his left arm, his right holding up a torch, in its aureole 'Liberty for the Oppressed' (O. P. Williams in the *New York Journal*); and 'The Message and the Messenger', showing Wilson at the rail of a ship gazing out at *Liberty* on his 4 December 1918 sailing to the European Peace Conference (C. H. Sykes, in the *Philadelphia Evening Ledger*) (p. 199).

15. The woodcut (*Harper's Weekly*, XXV [1881], 2 April, p. 216) bears the caption, 'Will it be necessary to erect an admonition of Pestilence and Death in our Harbor? A Question which our Citizens must Decide.' It accompanies an editorial (p. 211), 'The People and the Streets', occasioned by a citizens' meeting to censure the various ill practices that had fostered epidemics of scarlet fever, diptheria and outbreaks of smallpox, and political corruption that allowed 'drunken nurses and brutal attendants in the city institutions', specifically noting 'the decline of Central Park and the danger of insult to which women and children are exposed there'.

16. C. Oldenburg, *Proposals for Monuments and Buildings, 1965–9* (Chicago, 1969), Pl. 35. On *Liberty* and recent art, see M. Trachtenberg, 'The Statue of Liberty: Transparent Banality or Avant-Garde Conundrum?', *Art in America*, 62 no. 3 (May–June 1974), 36 ff. Not mentioned therein is Luis Jiminez' 1971–2 *Statue of Liberty*, a voluptuous, fiberglass, 7′ 3″ female with a flag between her legs (ill. S. Hunter, *American Art of the 20th Century* [New York, 1973] fig. 57).

17. Within the context of the film it is clear that in the final *montage* it is *Liberty* that kills the fascist villain. *Liberty* has also been the 'heroine' of a Broadway musical, *Miss Liberty* (a name acquired in 1916), book by Bob Sherwood, music by Irving Berlin (1948), perhaps compensation for her lights having been symbolically *out* during the war (cf. Chapter 7, n. 17).

18. In 1965, three black extremists (one of whom afterward hanged himself in jail) and a Canadian blonde were foiled in a nearly successful plot to blow off *Liberty*'s torch-arm (on 19 May one was quoted in the *New York Times*: 'if we could make that old girl blow her top, we'd really put a hurt on that old bitch'). In 1971, in protest against Vietnam a group of veterans peacefully occupied the statue for several days.

19. Gschaedler, op. cit., 161 ff. Such editions – monuments transformed into sculptural mementos for the masses – can be traced back to the Revolution, when reduced death masks of Marat and other heroes were sold in quantities (Licht, op. cit., 11); by mid-century the practice was widespread (Mirolli, op. cit., 21). In the case of *Liberty* the process has assumed grotesque proportions, with even large copies pandemic: several in Paris; Poitiers; in Times Square (1944–6) and at 43. W. 64th St. (55 feet high, or 1/3 scale, atop the Liberty Storage Co., 1902) in New York (cf. G. Talese, 'Miss Liberty Uptown', *New York Times*, Sunday magazine, 2 October 1960, 79 f.); Hiroshima (1947, on the site of a feudal castle destroyed by the bomb); in Hanoi (1/16th scale, for the Exposition of 1887 by the resident French general, a friend of Bartholdi [Betz, op. cit., 217]). Around 1950 a Kansas City manufacturer convinced the Boy Scouts to raise funds for 8 foot copies to be provided by a Chicago monument factory at $300 apiece, to be distributed in the Nation's parks 'to strengthen the arm of liberty'; by the time 60 of these had been executed and distributed to 22 states (with another 100 on order), the National Sculptural Society took offense at their inaccuracy (worse than the dollar models sold on Liberty Island) and created a public controversy (*Time*, 24 April 1950, with illustration).

Although losing out on this profitable endeavor, Bartholdi did not abandon dreams of further exploitation of *Liberty*. With the vision of numerous commissions in mind, in 1890 he wrote to Richard Butler (the American Secretary of the French-American Union): 'My idea has always been that it would be in the future a kind of Pantheon for the glories of American Independence; that you would build around the monument the statues of your great men and collect there all the noble memories. The island should become a sort of pilgrimage, a charming walk for the city.' (Gschaedler, op. cit., 113, 158 f.) Bartholdi may have envisaged peculiar company for *Liberty*, but one context in which the public tends to place the monument is no less jarring. A 1974 poll conducted by the U.S. Travel Service found *Liberty* named one of the 'seven man-made wonders of the U.S.A.' Her 'popularity' as such was above Hoover Dam, Disney World and Saarinen's Gateway Arch in St Louis (the last on the list) but below the Golden Gate Bridge (the first), Mt Rushmore and the Astrodome (*New York Times*, 27 January 1974 'Travel Section', p. 4).

20. Women (with the exception of Mme Bartholdi and Tototte de Lesseps) were not officially permitted to attend the unveiling ceremony, out of fear for their safety in the 'crush'. But the New York State Woman Suffrage Association hired a boat to cruise near *Liberty* during the ceremonies, on which speeches would be heard praising the embodiment of liberty as a woman, etc. (Gschaedler, op. cit., 137).

List of Illustrations

31. *Libertà*, monument to G. B. Niccolini. By Pio Fede, 1883. Florence, S. Croce. (Photo: Alinari.)

32. The Bartholdi family 'Helios' in Bartholdi's Paris study. From a photograph in the Musée Bartholdi, Colmar.

33. *Helios*. By J. Benk, 1876-8. Vienna, Naturhistorisches Museum. (Photo: Author.)

34. 'Soufflez, soufflez, vous ne l'éteindrez jamais'. By Grandville and Daumier. From *La Caricature*, 1835. Coll. W. Littel. (Photo: Author.)

35. *La République* or *La France éclairant le monde*. By Ange-Louis Janet-Lange, 1848. Paris, Musée Carnavalet. (Photo: Giraudon.)

36. *Commerce* and *Navigation*. By F. Jouffroy, 1861-4. Paris, Guichet du Carrousel, Palais du Louvre. (Photo: Author.)

37. *Notre-Dame de France*. Bronze, 16 m. high. By J. Bonnasieux, 1857-60. Le Puy-en-Velay. (Photo: Lys.)

38. *S. Carlo Borromeo*. Copper, 23.4 m. high. Designed by G. B. Crespi, 1610-96. Arona (Lago Maggiore). (Photo: Reggiori.)

39. *Religion*. Plaster 4 m. high. By Canova, 1814. Possagno, Gipsoteca. (Photo: Fondazione Cini.)

40. *Athena Parthenos*. Roman marble copy. Athens, National Museum.

41. *Faith*. Marble, 9 m. high. By Santo Varni, *c*. 1850. Genoa, Staglieno Cemetery. (Photo: Alinari.)

42. *Britannia*. Design by J. Flaxman, 1799. London, Victoria and Albert Museum. (Photo: Museum.)

43. *Hercules*. Copper, 9 m. high. By J. J. Anthoni, 1714-17. Base and cascade by G. F. Guernieri, 1701-18. Kassel, Park at Wilhelmshöhe.

44. *Monument to Frederick the Great*. Design by Friedrich Wilhelm IV, *c*. 1820-30. East Berlin, State Museum. (Photo by courtesy of Professor Dr Margarete Kühn.)

45. *Bavaria*. Bronze, 18 m. high. By L. Schwanthaler, 1837-48. Munich. (Photo: Marburg.)

46. *Arminius*. Copper, 26 m. high. By Ernst von Bandel, 1819-75. Teutoburger Wald. (Photo: Landesdenkmalamt Westfalen-Lippe.)

47. *Germania*. Bronze, 10 m. high. By J. Schilling, 1876-83. Rudesheim. (Photo: Author.)

48A. Kaiser Wilhelm Monument. By Bruno Schmitz, 1897. Koblenz. (Photo: Marburg.)

48B. *Völkerschlachtdenkmal*. By Bruno Schmitz, 1898-1913. Leipzig. (Photo: Marburg.)

49. *The Republic*. Plaster, 65 feet high. By Daniel Chester French, 1893. From a photograph taken at the Chicago Columbian Exhibition, 1893.

50. *La France couronnant Art et Science*. By Elias Robert, 1855. Palais de l'Industrie, Paris. (Photo: E.-D. Baldus, courtesy of Eastman House.)

51. *Truth*. By C.-V.-E. Lefebvre, 1859. Formerly Musée du Luxembourg, Paris.

52. Mrs Cornelius Vanderbilt as 'The Electric Light', 26 March 1883, photograph by Mora. (Courtesy of the New York Historical Society.)

53. New York Harbor, photograph of *c*. 1886-90. (Courtesy of the New York Historical Society.)

54. Immigrants' shipboard view of *Liberty*, woodcut from *Frank Leslie's Illustrated Newspaper*, 2 July 1887.

55. Map of New York Harbor. (Drawn by H. A. Shelley.)

56. *Liberty*, seen from a ship entering New York harbor. (Photo: Author.)

57. *Liberty*, seen from a ship entering New York harbor. (Photo: Author.)

58. *Liberty*. (Photo: National Park Service.)

59. *Lafayette*. Over-lifesize bronze, 1873-6. By Bartholdi. New York, Union Square. (Photo: New York Public Library.)

60. *Vercingétorix*. Bronze, 6 m. high. By Bartholdi, 1869-1903. Clermont-Ferrand. (Photo: Author.)

61. Gateway figure from the palace of Ashurnasirpal II at Nimrud, 883-859 B.C. London, British Museum. (Photo: Museum.)

62. Project for the *Statue of Liberty*. By Bartholdi, *c*. 1875. Colmar, Musée Bartholdi. (Photo: Author.)

63. 'The Colossus of Rhodes', engraving from J. B. Fischer von Erlach, *Historische Architektur*, 1721.

64. Liberty Island from the S. South-east, with New Jersey in the background, 1961. (Photo: Courtesy of the National Park Service.)

65. *Liberty* seen from Battery Park. (Photo: Author.)

66. Enlarging *Liberty*'s hand in plaster, 1876-81, with Bartholdi in the foreground, hatless. Photograph in Musée Bartholdi, Colmar.

67. *Liberty* in course of execution (repoussé process), 1876-81. From a photograph in the Musée Bartholdi, Colmar.

68. *Liberty* in course of execution (repoussé process), 1876-81. From a photograph in the Musée Bartholdi, Colmar.

69. *S. Carlo Borromeo*. (Photo: Reggiori.)

70. *Liberty*'s right hand and torch shown at the Philadelphia Centennial, 1876. From a photograph at the Musée Bartholdi, Colmar.

71. *Liberty*'s head shown at the 1878 Paris Exhibition, the exhibition building designed by Eiffel. From a lithograph at the Musée Bartholdi, Colmar.

72. The Pont du Garabit. By Eiffel, 1879-84. (Photo: Courtesy of H. R. Hitchcock.)

73. Preliminary project for the Tour Eiffel. Drawing by E. Nouguier and M. Koechlin of the Eiffel workshop, 6 June 1884. Eidgenössische Technische Hochschule, Zurich. (Photo: Courtesy of Professor Dr P. Dubas.)

74. Calculations for *Liberty*'s armature (polygon of forces) by Eiffel. From *Le Génie Civil*, 1883.

75. Calculations for the armature of *Liberty*'s arm by Eiffel. From *Le Génie Civil*, 1883.

76. Design for the armature of *Liberty*'s arm by Eiffel. From *Le Génie Civil*, 1883.

77. *Liberty*'s main armature in construction, 1881-4. From a photograph in the Musée Bartholdi, Colmar.

78. A and B. *Liberty* in course of construction, in Paris, 1881-4. From photographs in the Musée Bartholdi, Colmar.

79. Delivery of *Liberty* to the American Ambassador to France in Paris, 4 July 1884. From a contemporary woodcut in the Bibliothèque Nationale, Paris. (Photo: Author.)

80. View from the torch platform of *Liberty*. (Photo: Author.)

81. Interior view of *Liberty*, showing the linkage between trusswork and the statue. (Photo: Author.)

82. Interior view of *Liberty*, showing secondary trusswork and linkage to strapwork of the statue. (Photo: Author.)

83. Plans and cross-sections of *Liberty*'s armature and pedestal. From *Scientific American*, 1885.

84. Interior view of *Liberty*'s head. (Photo: Author.)

85. Interior view of *Liberty*'s head (looking towards the rear). (Photo: Author.)

86. Detail of 62. Pedestal probably after Viollet-le-Duc.

87. Pedestal project for *Liberty*. By Bartholdi, *c.* 1880. Colmar, Musée Bartholdi. (Photo: Author.)

88. Pedestal projects for *Liberty*. Probably by Bartholdi, 1882. Washington, D.C., A.I.A. Archive. (Photo: National Park Service.)

89. Pedestal project for *Liberty*. Probably by Bartholdi, 1882. Washington, D.C., A.I.A. Archive. (Photo: National Park Service.)

90. Pedestal project for *Liberty*. By R. M. Hunt, 1882-3. Washington, D.C., A.I.A. Archive. (Photo: National Park Service.)

91. Pedestal project for *Liberty*. By R. M. Hunt, 1882-3. Washington, D.C., A.I.A. Archive. (Photo: National Park Service.)

92. Pedestal project for *Liberty*, 'Pharos I'. By R. M. Hunt, 1883. Washington, D.C., A.I.A. Archive. (Photo: National Park Service.)

93. Model for *Liberty*'s pedestal, 'Pharos I'. By R. M. Hunt, 1883. Washington, D.C., A.I.A. Archive. (Photo: National Park Service.)

94. Casa de las Conchas, *c.* 1475. Salamanca.

95. The Pharos of Alexandria on an ancient coin. From T. E. Donaldson, *Architectura Numismatica*, 1859.

96. Model for *Liberty*'s pedestal, 'Pharos II'. By R. M. Hunt, 1883-4. Washington, D.C., A.I.A. Archive. (Photo: National Park Service.)

97A, B and C. Pedestal projects for *Liberty*. By R. M. Hunt, 1884. Washington, D.C., A.I.A. Archive. (Photos: National Park Service.)

98. Design for the definitive pedestal project. By R. M. Hunt, 1884. Washington, D.C., A.I.A. Archive. (Photo: National Park Service.)

99. Definitive pedestal project for *Liberty*. By R. M. Hunt, 7 August 1884. Washington, D.C., A.I.A. Archive. (Photo: National Park Service.)

100. *Liberty*'s pedestal. By R. M. Hunt, 1884-6. (Photo: Author.)

101. *Liberty*'s pedestal. By R. M. Hunt, 1884-6. (Photo: Author.)

102. *Liberty*'s pedestal, detail. By R. M. Hunt, 1884-6. (Photo: Author.)

103. Design for Washington Monument. By Arthur F. Mathews, 1879. Oakland, The Oakland Museum. (Photo: Museum.)

104. Pedestal project for *Liberty*. By R. M. Hunt, 1882-3. Washington, D.C., A.I.A. Archive. (Photo: National Park Service.)

105. The Ames monument. By H. H. Richardson, 1879 (relief by Saint-Gaudens). Sherman, Wyoming (a now vanished town near the golden spike of the transcontinental railroad). (Photo: Wayne Andrews, by courtesy of H. R. Hitchcock.)

106. Contribution certificate for the pedestal fund, *c.* 1883. Colmar, Musée Bartholdi. (Photo: Author.)

107. *Liberty* trophy in sterling silver, *c.* 1 m. high. Designed by J. H. Whitehouse for Tiffany & Co., 1886. Inscribed 'All Homage and Thanks to the Great Sculptor, Bartholdi' and 'A Tribute from the New York World and over 121,000 Americans to Auguste Bartholdi and The Great Liberty Loving People of France 1886'. Colmar, Musée Bartholdi. (Photo: Author.)

108. Fireworks celebrating the dedication of *Liberty*. From *The Illustrated London News*, 20 November 1886. (Photo: Author.)

109. First World War poster. Courtesy of the New York Historical Society, New York City.

110. First World War poster, 'Land of the Free and Home of the Brave', New York Public Library. (Photo: Author.)

111. Liberty Loan Poster, First World War. By Joseph Pennell. Museum of American Immigration. (Photo: Author.)

112. *Liberty* from a helicopter. Courtesy of American Airlines.

113. 'Will it be necessary to erect an admonition of Pestilence and Death in our Harbor?' from *Harper's Weekly*, 2 April 1881.

114. *Planet of the Apes*, 1967. Final scene. Courtesy 20th Century-Fox.

115. Advertisement for the film *Myra Breckinridge*, with Mae West, 1970.

116. 'What's a Nice Country Like You Doing in a State Like This, A Red White & Blue Revue'. Poster by J. Budne, New York, 1973.

117. Advertisement for the film *A Phantom of Liberty*, 1974.

118. *Liberty* exterior showing raised B in fold. (Photo: author.)

Index

Bold numbers refer to illustration numbers